Bebop by the Numbers

Book 1: Method, Exercises & Games

*a super fun, super simple way
to learn how to improvise...*

#465#243 `7215

by Danny Kolke

BebopByTheNumbers.com

For all the students and band directors who get up early every day to play this music, with love and gratitude...

Table of Contents

Introduction	7
Philosophy and Approach	9
Notation	11
#1 - Stingers	13
#2 - Pickups	15
#3 - Noodling	17
#4 - Simple Scales	21
#5 - Weaving	23
#6 - Looping	25
#7 - Circles	27
#8 - Turns	29
#9 - Stretching it Out	31
#10 - Blues Riffs	33
#11 - Shape Shifting	35
#12 - Diminished Shapes	41
#13 - Embellished Scale	49
#11 - Reading Chord Changes	51
Congratulations	65
Exercises	67
Exercising The Changes	85
Exercising Jazz Standards & Changes	87
Games	93
Bebop Prescription	100
Quick Reference Guide	101
Riff of the Day	102
Common Chord Progressions	104
About the Author	105
More Bebop	107

Introduction

So why Bebop by the Numbers? It started when I began teaching improvisation to beginning jazz band students and writing ideas for them to play on a whiteboard. It didn't take too long for me to get tired of writing every idea in three different keys. You see, band instruments are in different keys. I have no idea whose idea that was, but as a piano player, I find it fairly crazy. Regardless, I started writing ideas using numbers and told my band kids to figure out what each note was. Of course I would help them if they got stuck, but I was impressed at how quickly they could figure it out.

I also started using numbers to teach my piano students. Specifically talking about the different intervals of the chords and how to embellish the chord tones. I found it useful to talk about the ideas using numbers so my students could transpose them into different keys. I even incorporated using numbers into pedagogy exercises and methods for learning tunes.

Numbers are very helpful. If you can think about the numbers of the scale degrees instead of the letters, you can then translate ideas to different keys more quickly. "What's the one, what's the three?" And then in the other key, it's the same question, just a different answer. You can't transpose very quickly from one key to the other without using numbers.

I have also done a lot of experimenting with teaching students, testing who learned faster - the students who used notes and their corresponding letters, or the students who went by numbers? In my experience so far, the answer is "Numbers". Even though they may add an extra step and the students have to figure out how to play the pattern, they tend to learn more quickly, retain better and start coming up with their own ideas sooner than those who learn note by note. My theory is that it's necessary to make comparisons to play ideas. For example, "This is the minor third, and I'm going to the sixth, the sharp four, then five; I like that sound. Okay, let me try it with this key." I don't see students making those discoveries as quickly when we go note by note and ideas are written out for them.

So for these reasons, I am going to share with you Bebop by the Numbers.

Danny Kolke

Philosophy and Approach

I have been working with students of all ages for many years. During that time I have come to understand that everyone learns differently. Some people are visual and they need to see how it works. Some are auditory and need to hear it. Some need to feel it and touch their instrument to connect and feel the flow of the melody, scale, arpeggio, and create their own music.

Creating music is an artform. It can be very discouraging at times for the learner, trying to learn how to be creative. Like other artforms I have tried, sometimes I feel inspired to draw something, but it's just not right. It just doesn't look good to me. Well, music is the same way. We try and sometimes it just doesn't sound good to us.

I have been looking for ways to give specific advice to students and "that doesn't sound good" is just not constructive. Maybe the notes they played were perfect, but not in the right place to sound the way they want. Sometimes it's just putting the notes on the downbeat, and sometimes they need to add a couple more notes to help the line flow a little better for the style we are going for. What follows is the result of many experiments in teaching students, breaking apart the sounds of Bebop into smaller parts, and then reassembling them. Sort of a paint by numbers approach, but different. I wanted to be able to work with a student and say, "you have the bones of a great idea, try adding _____." I think my students and I, together, have come up with some building blocks that are pretty cool, and will help you develop musical ideas that consistently sound great.

In this method you are going to discover the building blocks for:

1. Creating Bebop ideas, lines, runs and melodies
2. Strategically placing them over chord progressions
3. Developing skills to create them in real time, and improvising in real time
4. Starting simple, creating the ability to go complex, and having the power to choose

In the next few pages, I will teach you the building blocks to create your own ideas. The rest is up to you. To get this style of music, you need to listen to it and work on your own dexterity. That is, your ability to play and place those ideas you are developing in spots that sound good.

This is not a method with all the answers, however it will take you to some pretty complex places and will help you become a very respectable jazz improviser. This method will enable you to get more complex and advanced in your approaches as our time on this creative journey goes on.

Everything in this method is cumulative in nature. Meaning that the first idea we're going to start with is a building block. The next idea adds on to that. Actually the first concept is the last concept. It's the ending of phrases. Yes, they can stand alone, but this first idea is often used as part of a larger phrase, and a larger idea. All of the concepts in this method follow that approach. And I challenge you as you work through them to add these ideas to each other and experiment with those sounds.

You may be asking, where did these concepts come from? Mostly these ideas have come from my transcriptions of solos, plus the melodies of popular bebop tunes. If you like the sounds of Charlie Parker, Dizzy Gillespie, Clifford Brown, Oscar Peterson, Gene Harris and others, these ideas and patterns should sound familiar to you. As I transcribed their phrases, I noticed common patterns, and I started to break those patterns into individual components that I could use to teach my students. The sounds we create in this method should be very familiar to you if you're listening to Jazz from that period, but these patterns are not exclusive to Jazz. I hear them everywhere, including classical music, and modern contemporary music. Maybe they are not assembled in the same way, nor played with the same swing feel, but a lot of these ideas and their embellishments are used in all forms of music.

Who is this book and method for?

This book is for anyone who wants to understand how to make music, but especially fans of Jazz.

If you are a beginner who can barely play your horn, you can start with the basic ideas in this book and see how far you can go. Each chapter adds to the skills in the previous chapter.

If you are a band director working with your students, this method can help you take your students through the building blocks of playing bebop. Start simple, and help them grow all the way to being able to play diminished bebop lines over chord progressions.

I debated how deep to go on the concepts. Maybe this material would be better suited broken up into different books? In the end I decided to keep true to the method I use when I work with my students. We start simple, and add on. We review, then add on some more. Each lesson we keep adding. And over time we get into some pretty cool and complicated stuff. During the whole journey, we keep trying to break it down and look for the simple ideas that connect it all. That is the same goal here with this book.

Any time that you need to tap out of this book and practice the ideas, go for it. Set down the book and come back to it later. Plus you can check out bebopbythenumbers.com for our growing library of tools to support this method.

Notation

Below is a quick guide to how we are going to use numbers in our notation of ideas. By default, we are using 8th notes in developing our bebop lines.

1 2 3 4 5 6 7 8 = normal scale tones, one through eight in the scale

9 10 11 12 13 = scale tones above the octave, i.e. same as **2 3 4 5 6**

7 = the 7th degree in the scale we are using, most commonly the major 7th

= raise the scale degree by a half step

b = lower the scale degree by a half step

**`** = play the scale degree below the 1st degree. i.e. `7 or `6 `7 1 2

So this means that **`6 `7 1 2 3** are the same notes as **6 7 8 9 10,** but one octave lower

_____ = play the scale degree long ie. `7_____ could be a half note or whole note, or a dotted something

(   ) = Notes grouped inside parenthesis are played over 1 beat, i.e. **(123)** = triplet

or **(1234)** = 16th notes

| = measure mark, mostly used to notate where the measure starts

, = eighth note rest

/ = quarter note rest

Bebop by the Numbers, Copyright 2023 Danny Kolke, Kolke Media LLC, All Rights Reserved

Notation FAQ's

What Do We Mean by Chord Tones?

Chords can get pretty complicated to understand. For our purposes we are going to focus mostly on simple chords built with scale tones **1**, **3** and **5**. These are also commonly called a *Triad*. Again, we will cover this more when we discuss Chord Progressions and Shape Shifting.

Minor vs Major 3rds

If you are playing an idea that has a **#2** and a **3** over a minor chord, change your idea to play the **3** as a **b3** and the **#2** as the natural **2**. Also, try a **b6** instead of the natural **6**, either can work depending on your preference. On diminished chords, do the same thing with the **b5** and the **#4**. We will cover this more when we discuss Shape Shifting and Chord Progressions.

#1 - Stingers

Stingers are *two eighth notes* that can be used to end your phrases. They also can stand alone by themselves. While Stingers can be made from many different notes, they always sound good when built with the 1, 3 or 5 of your scale. The 1,3 and 5 are the three notes that make up our basic chords, so we call them Chord Tones. Chord Tones can be played in any order.

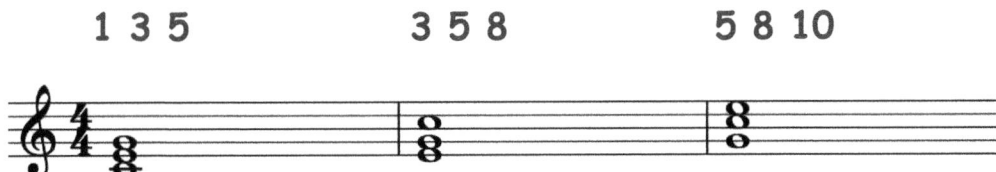

Note: *Stingers ALWAYS sound good. They can stand by themselves, or be part of a larger idea, and they can be placed on every beat.*

I prefer to write this out by just naming each Stinger by number:

3 1   3 5   1 5   5 8   3 8   1 3   5 3   5 1   1 8

Did I miss any combinations? You can try playing each one of these on each beat and the measure.

Tip: The biggest concept here is that we are ending on Chord Tones. Granted, you can end on other notes, but Chord Tones ALWAYS sound good. If you're worried about having your solo idea ending well, end it with a Stinger on a Chord Tone.

#2 - Pickups

A Pickup can be as simple as *one note added to the beginning of your idea*. Pickups can be longer by adding more notes to the front of your line. Like Stingers, Pickups could consist of many notes, and there is something that ALWAYS sounds good; a half step below your starting note, resolving up to your note, or, the Scale Tone above the note, and resolving it down. Both always sound good. What's a Scale Tone? Those are the notes in the scale you are playing. So 4 is above 3, 6 is above 5, etc.

Pickups + Stinger

#4 | 5   1

6 | 5 1

#2 | 3   1

4 | 3   8

#2 | 3   8

6 | 5   3

#2 | 3   1

`7 | 1   5

Add More Pickups

You can extend your Pickups with more half steps, for sure. Try *two note* Pickups.

Can you do half steps from above? It usually works well to start on the Scale Tone, and use two half steps.

Or three half steps.

#3 - Noodling

Noodling is what I call messing around with scale degrees by embellishing with half steps below the note. You can do it with any Scale Tone, but it always sounds great with Chord Tones.

Try Starting with the Embellishment of a Chord Tone

Note that we are starting with the embellishment, and then going to the Chord Tone. Try each one of these on a downbeat, and ending on the "And" of the beat.

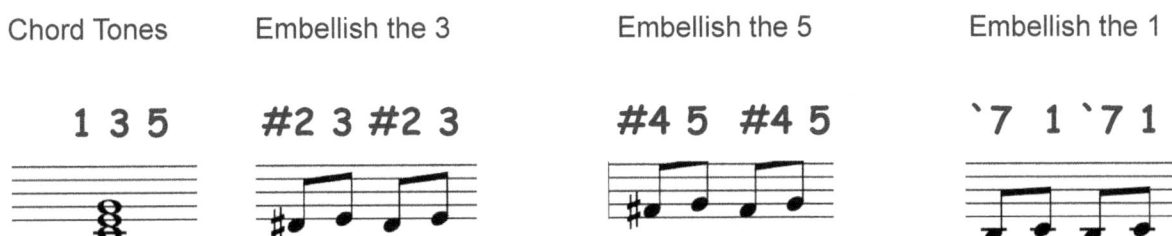

Of course these don't need to all be on beat 1. Try them on beat 2, 3 and 4 as well.

Mix and Match

Of course you can mix and match these and make longer lines.

#45 #45 #23 #23

And you can make longer patterns.

#4 5 #2 3 #4 5 #2 3 `7 1

`7 1 `7 1 #2 3 #2 3 #4 5

Try Starting on the Chord Tone, then Embellish

You can start on the Chord Tone and then move to your embellishment. Try doing this on the "offbeat" and play an odd number of notes, so your last note is a Chord Tone. Remember ending on a Chord Tone always sounds good.

5 | #4 5 #4 5 #23 #23| ‚ 5 #45 #23 #23

Noodling + Stinger

Try Noodling on your Chord Tones and adding a Stinger on the end.

```
 '7 1 '7 1    '7 1 '7 1   5 1
#2 3 #2 3   #2 3 #2 3   5 1
#4 5 #4 5   #4 5 #4 5   3 5


#4 5 #2 3    #4 5 #2 3    `7 1 3 1
`7 1 `7 1    #2 3 #2 3    #4 5 3 1
```

Pickup + Noodling + Stinger

Try with Pickups. If one Pickup, try it on the offbeat (the "And" of the beat). If two Pickups, try it on the "beat".

Offbeat:

```
 '7 | 1 '7 1  '7   1 '7 1 5
#2 | 3 #2 3 #2   3 #2 3 1
    5 | #4 5 #4 5   #4 5 #4 5   3 1
```

On the Beat:

```
| 3   4 #4 5 #2 3   #4 5 #2 3  `7 1 3 1
|`6 `#6 `7 1  `7  1   #2 3 #2 3  #4 5 3 1
```

Scale Tones

You can also Noodle on Scale Tones in your ideas. If we play a descending scale like this:

9 8 7 6 5

Then add our half step embellishments:

#8 9 7 8 #6 7 #5 6 #4 5

Stating the obvious, if you play this idea ascending, you are just playing a chromatic scale. There is nothing wrong with using that either. Just end on a Chord Tone.

2 #2 3 4 #4 5 #5 6 #6 7 8

Chromatic scales can be cool, especially with a Stinger.

#1 2 #2 3   4 #4 5 1

#4 - Simple Scales

When using scales to play bebop lines, we rarely play the whole scale straight through because we don't want our ideas to sound like a scale. We tend to break them into different sections and weave our ideas up and down through the scales. For this reason, I like to break scales into different sections, and then work on developing dexterity with different parts of the scale, so you can move around freely. I call these Simple Scales.

1 thru 5 = Lower scale,   4 thru 8 = Upper scale,   `6`7 1 2 3 = Middle   (aka 6 7 8 9 10)

1 2 3 4 5   4 5 6 7 8   `6`7 1 2 3   6 7 8 9 10

Practice them ascending (up) and descending (down).

1 2 3 4 5   4 5 6 7 8   `6`7 1 2 3   6 7 8 9 10
5 4 3 2 1,   8 7 6 5 4   3 2 1 `7 `6

Practice Up (ascending)

1 2 3 4, 2 3 4 5, 3 4 5 6, 4 5 6 7, 5 6 7 8, 6 7 8 9, 7 8 9 10

Practice Down (descending)

10 9 8 7, 9 8 7 6, 8 7 6 5, 7 6 5 4, 6 5 4 3, 5 4 3 2, 4 3 2 1

Simple Scales + Stingers

Add Stingers to the end of your Simple Scales, like so.

1 2 3 4 5 1   5 4 3 2 1 5   4 5 6 7 8 3   6 7 8 9 10 8

Pickups, Scales & Stingers

Put these concepts together: Try playing Pickups, with Simple Scales, and then add Stingers.

2 | 1 2 3 4 5 1

`7 | 1 2 3 4 5 3

5 | 4 5 6 7 8 3

4 | 3 4 5 6 5 1

#5 - Weaving

Our next concept also involves using scales to develop longer phrases. I call this Weaving. With Weaving, we move through scales, *back and forth on different parts of the scale.*

Weaving on the Lower Scale + Stinger

1 2 3 4 5 4 5 4   3   1

3 4 5 4 3 4 5 4   3   8

5 4 3 2   1 2 1 2   3   5

Weaving on the Upper Scale & Middle Scale

4 5 6 5 4 5 6 7   8 1

6 7 8 7 6 7 8 9   10 8

5 4 5 4 3 2 3 2   1 3

6 5 6 5 4 5 6 7   8 3

#6 - Looping

Looping is similar to Weaving: *jumping around and repeating parts of the scale* in order to extend our ideas. This is one way that we develop an ability to play runs. Again, you can jump to different parts of the scale, but jumping to Chord Tones almost always works great.

Loops + Stingers

1 2 3 4 5 3 4 5 3 1

1 2 3 4 5 3 4 5 6 7 8 5

1 2 3 4 5 3 4 5 3 4 5 6 5 3

1 2 3 1 2 4 3 5

You can Loop up or down.

2 | 1 2 3 4 5 8 7 6   5 4 3 2 3 4 5 3

6 | 5 8 7 6 5 8 7 6 5 3

You can combine Pickups, Looping and Weaving + Stingers

3 4 3 4 5 3 4 6   5 8 7 6 5 3

`7 | 1 2 3 4 5 3 4 5 6 8 7 6 5 3

2 | 1 2 3 4 5 3 4 5 6 8 7 6 5 4 3 2 3 5 3 1

#7 - Circles

Our next concept I call Circles because I use them to "Circle" around, and then land on a Chord Tone. Like Pickups, we are choosing a *half step below* or a *Scale Tone above* to make our Circles.

In the first 3 notes above I am going to the 5, but first I am going to start on the 6, then #4, Circling around the note I am going to and then resolving to the 5. I call this pattern Over Under because the first note is over (above) my destination note, and the second note is under (below). In the second example I start below the root on the 7, then play the 9, and then down to my root 8 (1). I call this pattern Under Over. The next two examples are #4, 6, 5 (Under Over) and then 2, `7, 1 (Over Under).

Circle Your Chord Tones

You can Circle your Chord Tones just like you would play an arpeggio, also known as a broken chord. Here are some of my favorite ways to play Circles. In each example, we are embellishing the third of our chord.

Under, Over
#243

Over, Under
4#23

Under Thru Over
#2343

Over Thru Under
43#23

Doubling up Under
#24#243

Doubling up Over
4#24#23

On Under Over (aka The Mona Lisa)
3#243

On Over Thru Under
34#23

Circles Can Go Anywhere

Note: You can double up Circles, and they also sound good with just a Stinger or by themselves.

Looping Circles

Looping Circles is also cool. Just repeat them in your patterns and maybe add a Stinger at the end.

Without a Stinger:

#2 4   3 #2 4 3   #2 4   3 #2   4 3

 , 6 | #4 5 6 #4   5 6 #4 5

With a Stinger:

#2 | 3 4 #2 3   4 #2 3 4   3 1

       #4 6 5 #4   6 5 #4 6   5 1

              4 #2 3 4   #2 3 4 #2   3 1

#8 - Turns

Turns enable you to add rhythmic embellishment and variety to your bebop lines. Like Pickups, Stingers and Circles, they work in multiple places to make your ideas more interesting.

Triplets & Sixteenth Note Turns

Two types of Turns to start with are triplets and sixteenth notes.

Triplet Pickups (3 half steps)

(3 4 #4) 5 3

(3 4 #4) 53 4#2 31

Triplet Arpeggios

(1 3 5) 78

(3 1 5) 78 #4 5

Add a Pickup

`7 |(1 3 5) 78 #4 5

Triplet Circles

(4 #2 3) 5 1

Triplet Loops

(#4 5 6)(#4 5 6) 53

(#2 3 4) (#234) 31

(`7 1 2) (`7 1 2) 35

16th Pickups
(454#2) 3 1

(2435) 4#2 31

16th Circles
(#456#4) 5 3

16th Arpeggios
(3 5 7 9) 8 5

16th Loops
(4542)(4542) 31

You can use Turns anywhere. I love using them at the end of my ideas, just before a Stinger.

34 #45   34# 45   (4 5 4#2) 3 1

/ (4 5 4 #2) 3 1   / (4 5 4 #2) 3 1

/ (b78 b75) 6 5   / (b78 b75) 6 5

/ (3 4 3 1) 2 1   / (3 4 3 1) 2 1

Pickup + 16ths + Stinger
, #2 (3 5 7 9)   8 5

2 - 16ths instead of 4
(, ,98) 8 5

2 - 16ths instead of 4
(, ,6#4) 53

2 - 16ths as a Pickup
(, ,4 #2) 34 #46 53

#9 - Stretching It Out

Adding long notes at the end of bebop lines can sometimes sound awkward. Instead, try adding them in the middle of your ideas, and add Stingers at the end. I call this "Stretching it Out."

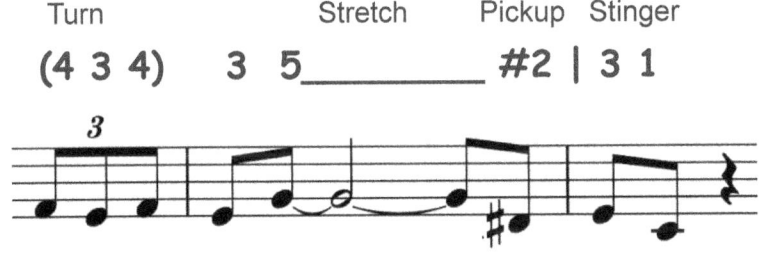

#10 - Blues Riffs

This feels like this is a good spot to insert my favorite simple blues patterns. I like to mix and match, and repeat (aka riff) these common patterns when I feel like playing a blues idea. Also, you can use them on all kinds of chord progressions, not just blues progressions.

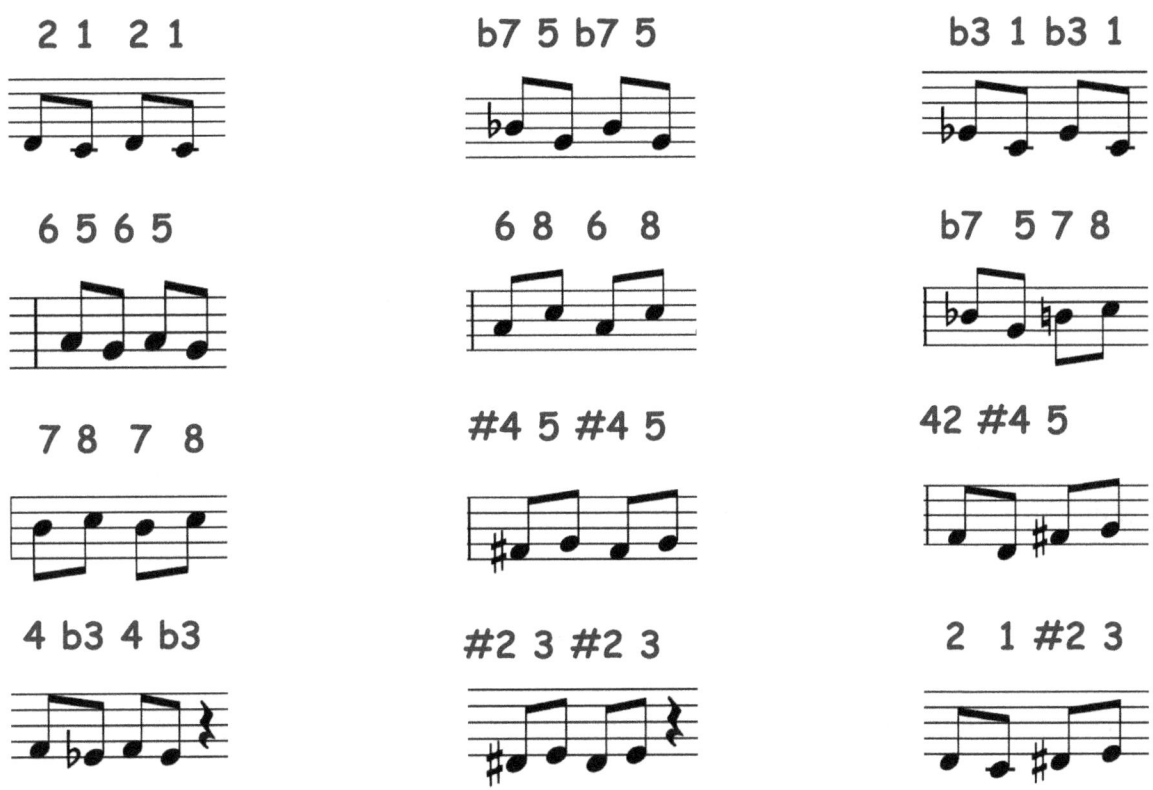

Blues Noodles & Embellishments

Just like we talked about in chapter 3 on Noodling, I like to Noodle on my chord tones in blues.

#4555 #4555   **#2333 #2333**   **`7111 `7111**

Blues Turns

Turns work great over blues, modifying the ideas we talked about at the start of this chapter. These are some of my favorites:

(2 b3 2 1) 2 1   (b78 b75) 7 8
(6 b7 6 5) 6 5   (4#4 4b3) 4 b3

Add Blues Turns to the end of your Blues Riffs

#4555 #4555 | (2 b3 2 1) 2 1
#4555 #4555 | (b7 8 b7 5) 7 8
#4555 #4555 | (4#4 4b3) 4 b3

Try these Five-Tone Scales for Blues Riffs

Ascending
1 2 b3 5 6 8
1 b3 4 5 b7 8

Descending
8 6 5 b3 2 1
8 b7 5 4 b3 1

Now Put Them Together

Try them with different combinations as well as repeating patterns over and over again.
We call this *riffing*.

#4555#4555|(4#4 4b3) 4b3 / /| #4555#4555|(4#4 4b3) 4b3 / /

(2 b3 2 1) 2 1 / / |(2 b3 2 1) 2 1 / / |(2 b3 2 1) 2 1 / /

4343 / / | 4b34b3 / / | 4343 / / | (4#4 4b3) 4 b3

2121 6565 4b3 4b3

6565 6565 b75 78

7888 7888 (b7 8 b7 5) 7 8

1 2 b3 5 6 8 / / | (b7 8 b7 5) 7 8

#45 #45 4b3 4b3 | (b7 8 b7 5) 7 8

#11 - Shape Shifting

As you improvise over chord changes, you will notice how chords change their shapes during the form of a song - for example, from major to minor, or from a major 7 to a dominant. It's important to understand how to change the shapes of your ideas to match major, minor, diminished, dominant and other sounds.

Lower Scale Shapes

Major Chord
1   3   5
1 2 3 4 5

Minor Chord
1   b3   5
1 2 b3 4 5

Diminished Chord
1   b3   b5
1 2 b3 4 b5

What to do with this?

When a chord that is major changes to minor (with the same root), you would flat the 3rd degree in your patterns that you play. If it's a diminished chord, you would flat both the 3rd and the 5th degrees. When you go back to major, the opposite is true and you would raise from a b3 to a natural 3rd, and natural 5th.

Shape Shifting Between Chord Types

Play over a chord as it shifts between major and minor, changing between a b3 and a natural 3.

| 1234 53 / | 12b34 5b3 / | 3123 / / | b312b3 / / |
| I | i-7 | I | i |

Play over a chord as it shifts between major and diminished, changing between a b3 and a natural 3, and the b5 and natural 5.

| 1345 43 / | 1b34b5 4b3 / | 3123 / / | b312b3 / / |
| I | i° | I | i° |

Notice how little changes between chords. Minor and diminished both share the flat 3rd, and diminished flats the 5. But these differences define the sounds of the song, and it's important to play those differences.

> Tip: You can start simple with focusing on shapes around the basic 1 3 and 5 of the chords, and once you are comfortable with that, start exploring the "Upper Scale Shapes" and other extensions or embellishments to chords.

Upper Scale Shapes

Shapes don't only shift on the triads (135's) of our chords. They also change on the notes above the 5, or what I call the Upper Scale Shapes.

Notice how many of these are the same shape, and how the 7th and 6th are the only thing that changes.

Major
4 5 6 7 8

Natural Minor
4 5 b6 b7 8

Dominant
4 5 6 b7 8

Melodic Minor
4 5 6 7 8

Harmonic Minor
4 5 b6 7 8

Minor 7
4 5 6 b7 8

Half Diminished
4 5 6 b7 8

> How about "Fully Diminished?" We are going to cover fully diminished upper scales and patterns in our next lesson, chapter 12. Half diminished chords Upper Scale shapes are the same as minor 7th chords.

Minor Stingers

Stingers with just 1's and 5's are no different in *minor chords* than with *major chords*. Patterns with 3's are different in *minor*.

b35   **5b3**   **b3 8**   **8b3**   **1b3**   **b31**

Diminished Stingers

The b3 and 1 patterns with Minor Stingers are the same as *diminished*. The difference between *minor* and *diminished* is the b5. Diminished Stingers have both a b3 and a b5.

1b5   **b3b5**   **b5b3**   **b51**   **b58**

Yes you can play b3 1 stingers over a diminished chord, and you don't *have to* play the b5.

b3 8	**b3 1**	**1 b3**

Minor Pickups & Stingers

Half step below and *Scale Tone* above pickups with *minor*.

,`7 1 b3	,2 b3 5	,2 | b3 1	,#4 | 5 b3

, 2 b3 8	, 7 8 b3	,2 1 b3	,4 b3 1

, 4 b3 5	, 4 b3 8

Either the 6 or b6 can work as the *Scale Tone* above depending on what sound you prefer. It may depend on the song you are playing and what works best.

,6 5 b3	,b6 5 3	,b6 5 b3	,b6 5 8

Diminished Pickups & Stingers

Diminished 1 b3 patterns are the same as *minor*. Patterns on the b5 are different.

,b6 b5 b3	,b6 b5 8	,4 b5 b3	,4 b5 8	,4 b5 1

Minor Noodling

Noodles are different on the b3 in a *minor* chord vs *major*. The half step below is the 2, and the *Scale Tone* above is the 4.

b2 3 b2 3 b2 3 b2 3 | 5 1

4 b3 4 b3 4 b3 4 b3 | 5 1

Diminished Noodling

Like Pickups, it is the b5 that is different in Diminished Noodling vs minor. Try the 4 to the b5 from below, and the b6 to the b5 from above.

4 b5 4 b5 4 b5 4 b5 | b3 1

b6 b5 b6 b5 b6 b5 b6 b5 | b31

Minor Circles

Minor Circles work great. Use the 2 for the half step below the b3, the 4 from above the b3. For the 5, you can try either the 6 or the b6 depending on the sound you prefer.

Minor Circles on the 3

Under, Over
24 b3

Doubling up Under
24 24b3

Over, Under
42 b3

Doubling up Over
42 42 b3

Under Thru Over
2b3 4b3

On Under Over
b32 4b3

Over Thru Under
4b3 2b3

On Over Thru Under
b34 2b3

Minor Circles on the 5

Minor patterns with the 65 are the same as major 65, unless you flat the 6. Both work over minor chords.

Under, Over

#4 6 5

#4b6 5

Over, Under

6#4 5

b6#4 5

Under Thru Over

#45 65

#45 b65

Over Thru Under

65 #45

b65 #45

Doubling up Under

#4b6 #4b6 5

#4b6 #4b6 5

Doubling up Over

6#4 6#4 5

b6#4 b6#4 5

On Under Over

5#4 65

5#4 b65

On Over Thru Under

56 #45

5b6 #45

How about minor & diminished Weaving & Looping? Sure, all of the ideas we have been discussing can work on those scales. In the next chapter we are going to get into diminished scales and patterns.

#12 - Diminished Shapes

Diminished shapes are a common form of embellishment used not just in Jazz improvisation, but in many genres of music. We are going to explore some simple ways to add diminished ideas into your playing. Let's start with understanding how to use diminished over major Key Centers.

Let's start with a basic *major scale* playing from 1 thru 9 and back down.

With a major chord, the first way I like to start adding *Diminished Shapes* is by *flatting* the 6th note of the scale.

Next, I also like to sharp that same note and play them together, with both a #6 and b6.

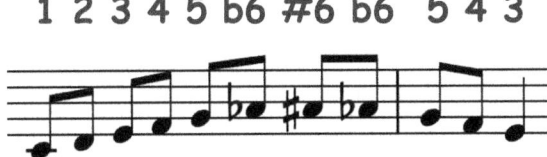

To keep extending that *Diminished Shape*, I will add the 7, and sharp the 8 (aka the *octave*). Note that I call it the sharp 8, because I don't play the regular 8 in this scale.

If we start on the 2nd note in our scale, and play through the 9th, we have a diminished scale. This is commonly referred to as a *whole - half diminished scale*.

2 3 4 5 b6 #6 7 #8 9

> Why do I teach diminished this way? Because this is where they work really well on major *Key Centers*. I will play this over major chords all the time. I can start in the Key Center, go to *Diminished Shapes* and come back to my Chord Tones. I just love the way it sounds. Sometimes I will end it on the 9th, just like the scale example above.

Now What? Try Stingers & Other Stuff

Add Stingers to *Diminished Shapes*.

#8 7 #6 b6 5 3

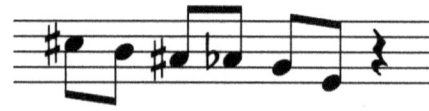

5 b6 #6 7 #8 7 #6 b6   5 3

Noodling + Stinger

#4 5 #4 5   5 b6 #6 7   #8 7 #6 b6   5 3

Weaving + Stinger

5 b6 5 b6 #6 7 #6 7   #8 7 #6 b6   5 3

Looping + Stinger

5 b6 #6 7 5 b6 #6 7   #8 7 #6 b6 #8 7 #6 b6   5 3

Diminished on Minor

When playing Diminished ideas on a minor chord, play the b5 b6 and natural 6 and 7.

1 2 b3 4 b5 b6 6 7 8

7 6 7 6 b6 b5 b6 b5 4 2 b3 1

4 b5 b6 6 7 6 b6 b5 b6 b5 4 2 b3 1

b3 4 b5 b6 6 7 6 b6 b5 4 b3

Diminished on Dominant

When playing Diminished ideas on a *dominant 7 chord*, flat the 2, sharp the 2 and the 4, and flat the 7th.

1 b2 #2 3 #4 5 6 b7 8

#4 5 6 b7 6 5 #4 5

1 b2 #2 3 #2 b2 1 5

8 b7 8 b7 6 5 6 5 #4 3 #4 3 5 1

Diminished Shortcut

Which diminished scale should you play? Find out what *key** you are in, and start on the 2nd degree of your scale.

2 3 4 5 b6 #6 7 #8 9

2 3 2 3 4 5 4 5 b6 #6 b6 #6 7 #8 7 #8 9

Or go to the 5th scale tone, and up a half step (b6). It's the same scale. We are just starting in a different place.

5 b6 5 b6 5 4 3

5 b6 #6 7 #6 7 b6 5 4 3

Ascending:

2 3 2 3 4 5 4 5 b6 #6 b6 #6 7 #8 7 #8 9

Descending:

#8 7 #8 7 #6 b6 #6 b6 5 4 5 4 3 2 3 2

Did you say, "find out what key we are in?"

Oops. Reading chord changes and knowing what keys we are in are important topics that we are going to introduce in chapter 14, if you are ready for it. If you aren't ready for that, no biggie. The ideas in this method up until this point will work if you play them over the chords in your songs, major, minor, diminished and dominant chords. Just remember to end on Stingers!

Some Diminished Scale Tricks

Not everyone learns the same way, especially diminished scales. Some people can easily learn diminished scales alternating whole steps and half steps, like this.

Whole - Half = W H W H W H W H

Half - Whole = H W H W H W H W

Then learn those two patterns starting from each note in the chromatic scale. Right?

Some people struggle with that method. Me included, until I discovered that the pattern repeats after 3 notes. And from that point on, it's the same exact scale just starting in a different place. I only needed to learn 3 scales.

Yes, there are only 3 diminished scale patterns. If you learn how to play them starting on different notes, (just like inversions of chords, or modes of scales), there are only 3 patterns that you have to learn to know all your diminished scales.

Whole - Half vs. Half - Whole

If you learn the patterns, the difference is just which note you start on.

Whole - Half = 2 3 4 5 b6 #6 7 #8 9

Half - Whole = 3 4 5 b6 #6 7 #8 9 10

Or take your Whole - Half, and add a Half Step pick-up in front of it.

Whole - Half = 2 3 4 5 b6 #6 7 #8 9

Half - Whole = #1 2 3 4 5 b6 #6 7 #8 9

If you learn these patterns starting on C, C# and D, you will have learned the pattern for all 12 Whole - Half diminished scales, and all 12 half - whole diminished scales. There are only 3, then notes and patterns repeat. Where you start within the pattern, and playing the same exact notes, will determine which scale it is called.

Two Minor 4 Note Scales a #4 or b5 Apart

Here's a good trick I learned from my teacher and jazz pianist Bob Nixon. Instead of trying to learn whole - half, whole - half, etc., try playing 4 notes of a minor scale, then go up a half step and play 4 notes of that minor scale, then up a half step, and you are back at the scale you started with.

D minor + Ab minor

Db minor + G minor

C minor + F# minor

If you add a *half step Pickup* below each of those scales, those are your half - whole diminished scales, and you will have learned all 24 diminished scales, starting in the same spot of course.

If you loop and weave them, you will be able to play them starting on different notes too.
Remember that there are only 3 of them, and then the pattern repeats.

#13 - The Embellished Scale

Up until this point, we have been focused on using embellishments with Chord Tones. You can also use half step embellishments to your Chord Tones with your scales to develop new ideas and patterns. This scale is using half steps on 1 3 5 and 7s, our Chord Tones.

Major Scale

Embellished Major Scale

Note that we are starting on the embellishment for our 1, and adding embellishments for 3,5 and 7.

Try Weaving and Looping with the Embellished Major Scale

Try These With Your Embellished Scale

Stingers

`712#2 35

`7|12#23 4#456 51

Noodling + Stinger

`71`71 #234#4 51

Looping + Stinger

`712#2`712#2 31

Looping + Circle + Stinger

`712#2 34#45 34#46 51

Weaving and Looping + 98 Stinger

`712#2 312#2 34#45 #456#6 7898

#14 - Reading Chord Changes

There are two really important concepts that come next that will help you understand how chords are related to each other in the music we are playing. These concepts are understanding what key you are in, and understanding what the chord progression is. Understanding both will help you create ideas that sound good with these chords.

Important: If you feel like you are not yet ready for this topic, you can skip this chapter and come back to it at another time. You can still apply everything you have learned so far in Bebop by the Numbers and create great sounding music.

What Key Are You In?

All notes belong to a key, their chords, and their scales. All notes belong to more than one key, but not every note is in every key. Let's look at major keys first.

Major Keys

There are 7 notes in a scale in a major key, and 12 notes total in a chromatic scale. That means that 5 of those 12 notes are not in the major key we are playing in. Each note in the scale is also called a scale degree (aka Scale Tone). A chord built on top of a scale degree is also called the "number" of that scale degree, plus its defining characteristics. ie. One Major, Two Minor, Four Major, etc.

Building Simple Chords

One simple way to build chords is to play then skip every other note in a scale.

1 + 3 = 3rd
1 + 3 + 5 = Triad
1 + 3 + 5 + 7 = 7th Chord
1 + 3 + 5 + 7 + 9 = 9th Chord

If you move up the scale, play a note and skip a note, you will build these chords.

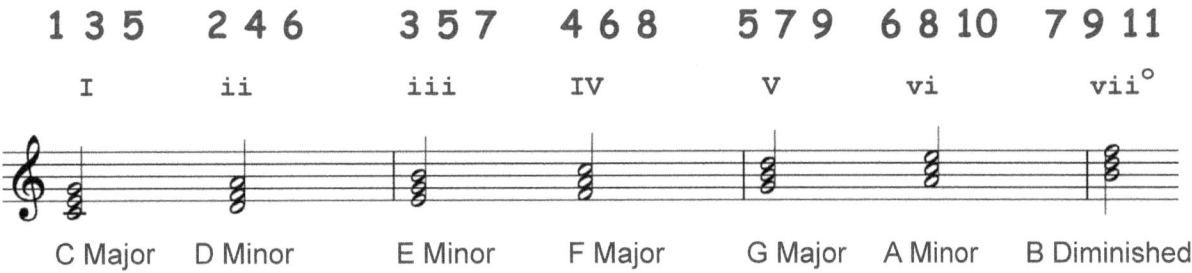

These are the chords native to the key we are playing in, with no alterations, extensions or embellishments. In this example, the key of C.

> Tip: Note that we are using Roman Numerals for our chord notation. Uppercase indicates a major third in the chord, lowercase means minor 3rds, and **o** indicates diminished. Diminished has a minor third and a diminished 5th. Some musicians call it a minor fifth instead of diminished 5th. If you are new to Roman Numerals here is a quick lesson.
>
> $$i=1 \quad ii=2 \quad iii=3 \quad iv=4 \quad v=5 \quad vi=6 \quad vii=7$$
> $$I=1 \quad II=2 \quad III=3 \quad IV=4 \quad V=5 \quad VI=6 \quad VII=7$$

Seventh Chords that are Native to Major Keys

If we add the 7th to each chord we get the following progression on our Scale Tones.

1 3 5 7, 2 4 6 8, 3 5 7 9, 4 6 8 10, 5 7 9 11, 6 8 10 12, 7 9 11 13

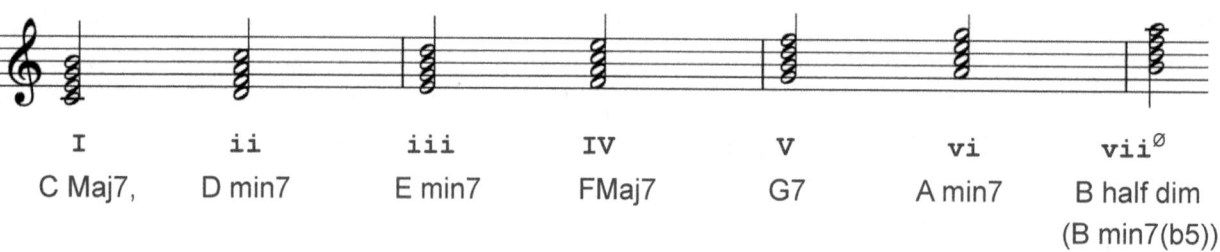

| I | ii | iii | IV | V | vi | vii⁰ |
| C Maj7, | D min7 | E min7 | FMaj7 | G7 | A min7 | B half dim (B min7(b5)) |

All these chords, and notes within them, are all "Diatonic." This means that they all contain the natural, unaltered notes in the key we are in. In this example, the key of C.

Understanding the Math & Playing the Odds

How many of each type of chord are there in a major key?

- There is only 1 dominant 7th chord.
- Only 1 half diminished chord.
- There are 3 minor 7th chords.
- There are 2 major 7th chords.
- This is true for ALL major keys.

What Odds am I talking about?

If I am playing a song in a major key, and I see a dominant chord, odds are that it's a **v** chord (aka Dominant 7th). If I see a major 7th chord in a song, odds are it's either the **I** chord or the **IV** chord. If I see a minor 7th chord, it's probably a **ii**, **vi**, or a **iii**.

If I see a half diminished chord, odds are it's the `vii°`, and we are changing keys to the relative minor. (Whoa now! We'll come back to this one later).

More of this Odds Stuff

If I see a dominant chord that is *not on the 5th degree of the scale*, the odds are that I am changing keys in the song. Maybe not for the entirety of the song, but *maybe it's just for a phrase*.

The same is true if I see a minor chord not built on the 2,3 or 6th degree. Odds are I am changing keys, at least for a bit.

What's the Chord Progression?

Chord progressions support the melodic structure of our songs and create opportunities for harmonies and counter melodies. Chord progressions make music more interesting.

For example, here is a simple idea where all of these notes are in the key of C.

Not only are all of those notes in the C scale, they are also in the chords in the key of C. In fact, in this simple idea we are playing every note in the key of C. We can play this idea over a C chord and that would work just fine. However, if we want to add more variety to our music we can change chords.

This creates new harmonic opportunities for embellishments and resolutions. So even though this idea would fit over a C major chord, these notes are also used in other cords. In fact, there are a bunch of chords that live naturally in the key of C major.

Here is the same idea with three different sets of chord changes, all ending on C major 7.

This idea does not have to end on a C major 7 chord either. It could end on the 4 chord (F major) or the 6th (A minor), like so:

Which chord progression is correct? Good question. It really depends on the harmonies that the composer is creating with the song. All of them can work, and here's the good and bad news; many more combinations are possible. Do you have to know them all? No. But it does help to be familiar with common chord progressions and understanding how the sounds change as you see these types of chords. I call this "Shape Shifting." I look for how the chords shift the shape of the notes that I am playing. For example, my B natural may become a Bb for a few measures, or my F natural, an F sharp.

What to Look for?

Start with some basic questions?

- Is one of the chords the same as my *key signature*?
- Is there a major 7 chord at the start or end of my phrase?
- Are these chords that I am looking at in the same key or scale?
- Is one of them a dominant 7th chord?
- Does it feel like we are changing keys?

Let's apply this to a very simple and common *chord progression*.

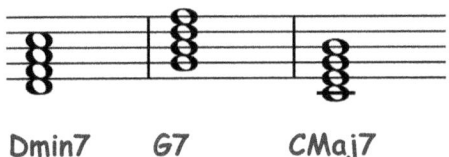

Dmin7   G7   CMaj7

Hypothesis:
- I see a C major 7.
- Are all these chords in C major?
- Is C major my Key Center? Is the root of each chord in the same scale?
- Is the chord native to that Key Center, or is it modified?

In this example, the answer is "yes." All these chords are in the key of C.
This is a `ii V I` in the *key of C*.

What's the Point here?

What's the point? It gives me more options to play, if I know that these chords are leading to another chord. I can play D minor ideas, and G ideas and then C major ideas. ***I can also play C major riffs over the entire phrase***. Both of these approaches will work! How cool is that?

This concept is very important. Read that last paragraph again please!

Let's do some more Common Examples

Chord Progression
| C Maj7 | D min7 G7 | C Maj7 | G min7 C7 | FMaj7 |

Hypothesis. I see major 7th chords. Does this phrase start in C major and then change to F major? We know from the previous example that D minor 7 and G7 are in C, but what about the F major 7? F major 7 is in the key of C. It's the `IV` chord. What about the 2 chords before that? G is normally a major triad in the key of C. Making it minor gives it a Bb instead of a B natural. G is the 2nd degree in the F scale, and C is the 5th degree in F. Also, the C chord is now dominant instead of a major 7th chord. This looks like a `ii V I` (2 5 1) in the key of F major. We have shifted from C as our Key Center to F.

Chord Progression:

| C Maj7 | D min7 G7 | C Maj7 | Gmin7 C7 |
| F Maj7 | D min7 G7 | C Maj7

Continuing our example, it looks like we are going back to a C major 7, and this is a familiar chord progression, D minor 7, G7, C. Is the D minor in the key of F major? Yes, it's the 6th. D is also the 2 in the key of C. Is the G7 in the key of F, or C? It has that B natural, making it major, and it's dominant, meaning it's the 5 of something. G7 is the v7 (5) of C. In this example, we start in C major, temporarily go to F major, and then come back to C major.

Chord Progression

C Maj7	D min7 G7	C Maj7	G min7 C7	
F Maj7	D min7 G7	C Maj7	A7	
D min	G7	C	D min G7	

We now have added an A7 in measure 8 after our C major 7. Is the root of the A7 in the key of C? Yes it is. Is A normally a dominant chord in the key of C? No, it's normally minor. This means that the 3rd of this chord is raised from the normal minor 3rd, to a major 3rd. That note is a C#. And since this chord is dominant, A7 is the 5th degree of what key? It's the key of D. Our next chord is a D, but not a D major, it's minor. So this looks like a very temporary shape shift to D minor, which then quickly turns into a recognizable pattern, our D minor, G7, C. I know when I am playing this that I want to grab that C# in my soloing.

> **Tip: Minor Chords**
>
> When looking at minor chord progressions it's helpful to use *harmonic minor* as your default scale. For this scale, we raise the 7th degree in our key signature to be a major 7th. Or when compared to a major scale with the same root, it looks like we lower the 3rd and the 6th. That gives us a minor 1 triad, and a minor 4 triad, but a major 5th triad.
>
> Major Scale =   1 2   3 4 5   6 7 8
>
> Harmonic Minor =   1 2 b3 4 5 b6 7 8

Let's Do This Again

Chord Progression:

| C min7 | F7 | Bb Maj7 | Eb Maj7 | A-7(b5) | D7 | G-7 | |

Hypothesis: I see a dominant F7 chord, then a Bb major 7. Is Bb major a Key Center? After the Bb, I have an Eb major 7. Eb is the 4 chord in the key of Bb. Is this another "temporary shift" in Key Centers? After the Eb, I have an A-7(b5), aka a half diminished chord, and then I see another dominant chord. This time a D7, which is in the key of G. I do have a G chord after that, but it's minor, not major. So is G minor another Key Center? Yes. This phrase starts with a `ii V I` (251) in Bb, goes the 4 chord, and then a `ii V i` (251) in G minor. Bb and G minor share the same key signature, and this type of shifting between a major and its relative minor is very common in many genres of music.

How About The Blues?

There are songs that have a dominant Key Center, like the blues. In this example you will see that there are no major 7 chords, and everything is dominant. Do the same rules apply?

Blues Chord Progression Version 1

C7	F7	C7	
F7		C7	
G7		C7	

In this classic blues form, it's common to treat each chord as a Key Center, while making sure to add the dominant 7th in our riffs and ideas since it is also a Chord Tone. That means we will play ideas in C, F and G. It's also common to use the end of each phrase to lead into the next Key Center. For example, in measure 4 start playing ideas that lead into the F7, like maybe a `ii V I`, in the key of F.

Blues Chord Progression Version 2

C7	F7	C7	G min C7	
F7		C7	A7	
D min7	G7	C7 A7	D-7 G7	

In this version of the blues, C is definitely our main Key Center, and we go to F right away and then back to C. In measure 4 we see a `ii V` leading us into the key of F in measure 5. Measure 8 we see a dominant A7, which leads us to a D-7 in our last phrase, a `ii V I` (251) in the key of C. The last

2 measures start on C and do what we call a turnaround. This is a very common turnaround, `I VI7 ii V` then back to `I` (1) for the top of the form.

Minor Key Center Math

Let's pick the key of C minor. C minor has 3 flats just like Eb major. C minor is the "Relative Minor" of Eb. If we play the C natural minor scale, we get the following.

Note that our half steps have shifted their location in our scale. They are now between the 2 & 3 and the 5 & 6. In a major scale they are between 3 & 4 and 7 & 8. This makes sense because we are playing the same notes as an Eb major scale, just starting in a different spot. This is also called the "Aeolian Mode." If we play our 7th chords we get the following.

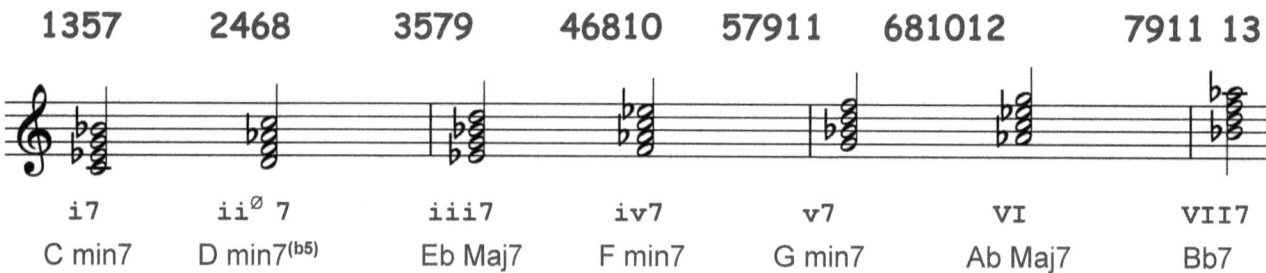

Is this New Math?

Our math is the same as in a major scale, but the location of our minor and major chords have shifted. One, four and five are now minor sevens, three and six are major sevens, two is half diminished, and the chord on the seventh degree is now dominant. Just like a major scale, there are still 3 minor 7's, 1 half diminished, 2 major's and 1 dominant. But here's the trick, the five chord in natural minor, is minor with a minor 3rd. Most genres of music tend to prefer a five chord with a major third in it. This is because of how it sounds when it resolves back to the one chord. As a result, it is common and even preferred to raise the third of that 5 chord. The note we end up raising is the 7th note of the scale. Yes, this also gives us the *harmonic minor scale*. If we play our chords and modify ONLY the five chord, raising that note we get the following.

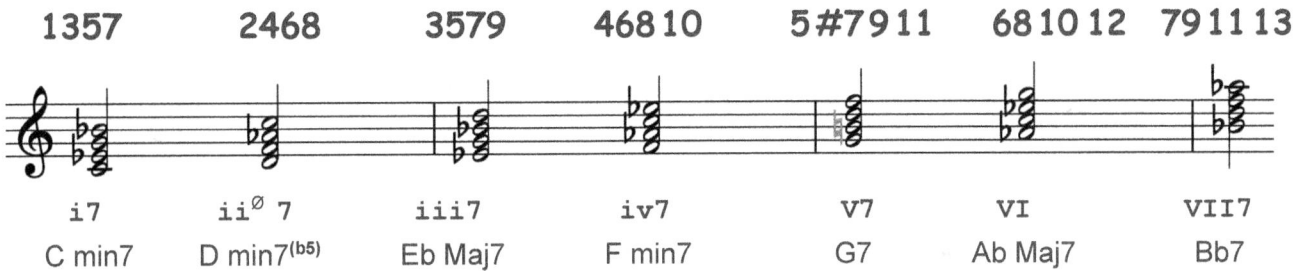

Please note that on the 5 chord (V7) I wrote a #7 because we are raising the 7. While it's true that in Eb we are making it a natural instead of a flat, this is not true for all keys. The practice is to raise that note, hence the sharp.

> Tip: I prefer to play natural minor for most of my lines, and then use my embellishments on my chord tones. This also gives me that natural 7th whenever I want it. When I am thinking in a minor key, I default to a major 3rd on my five chord.

Minor Two Five One Progressions

Note that the two chord in a minor scale is half diminished (aka *minor 7 b5*). We raise the 3rd on the 5 chord to give us dominant. The 9th on that dominant in our Key Center is a b9, and the one is minor. So the default two five one progression in a minor Key Center is:

ii7(b5)   V7(b9)   i7

D-7(b5)   G7(b9)   C-7

What? There are Two Dominants, the Five and the Seven?

The seven chord in the natural minor scale is dominant, unless you choose to raise the root, *(like the harmonic minor scale)*. This would make it a *fully diminished chord*. Depending on what you want to play, they both often work and this becomes something you can choose to play at your discretion. It's however you want to sound.

Four Minor, Seven Dominant, Three Major

If you are in a minor key and see the progression iv VII7 III (4 minor, 7 dominant, 3 major 7), remember that these are the same chords as a two five one in the relative major. Odds are that you are changing Key Centers to the relative major when this happens.

Keep it Simple, Play the Key Centers

It's easy to go a little crazy on all this music theory stuff. The important thing to understand is why we are talking about it.

We want to understand what key we are in, phrase by phrase. Then we can start by playing ideas over that Key Center. This is often a great way for beginners to play chord changes and sound good.

And as professionals, we use this information to build lyrical ideas that connect across different chords and connect with our Key Centers and transitions between them.

Shape Shifting Over Chord Progressions

Next we are going to take two different approaches to come up with the same exact notes. This illustrates that there are different ways you can approach playing over chord progressions, and *still end up playing the same notes.*

Ex 1. Thinking Chord by Chord

In this first example, with each chord we are resetting numbers, and using the scale tones of the chord.

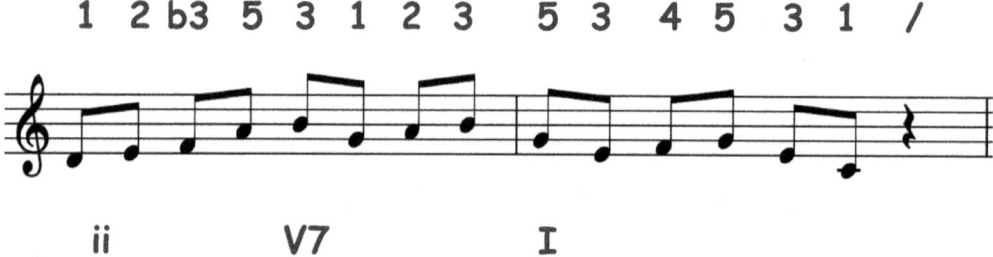

Ex 2. Thinking in the Key Center

In this example, we are going to think of the ii V I in a key of I, playing the notes in the scale of I.

So what's the "correct" approach? Should you think chord by chord, or identify the key centers and play those? They both work. I do think it's helpful to try both. I personally think that knowing how your song shifts to different Key Centers is especially helpful in developing your improvised ideas. We are going to look at that with our next examples.

Shape Shifting to Different Keys

Noticing how chords change their shape from measure to measure, and how songs change shape and transition from one key center to another, will give you a lot of options for creating cool ideas, and placing those ideas in the right spot to match those changes.

In this example, we are going to look at a common progression; changing from a key center on the I chord, to the IV chord. In the process of this change, our V goes from major to minor, and our I chord becomes a dominant chord, which is the V of our IV chord.

Ex 4. Thinking In the Key of One

In this example we are playing the idea in the key of I, and shifting the notes when we change keys in measure 3 and 4. To make it work, we are flatting the 7th, and emphasizing the 4th and 6th degrees, because they are 1 and 3 of the IV chord.

Ex 5. Thinking In the Key of One then Four

Now let's look at the same ideas, but with their numbers represented in two different key centers, the I then the IV. Note: ii/IV means the ii chord in the key of IV, etc.

Common Notes in Different Chords

Tip: You can look for notes that are shared in different chords and choose those notes as key themes in your ideas. For example these chords:

Dmin7   G7(b9) | CMaj7

Contain these notes:

D F A C   G B D F | C E G B

You could try embellishing the D and F, then resolving to the C and E in the third chord. This is one of many possible approaches. D is also the 9th in a C major 7 and you could try resolving to that note.

Playing Diminished Over Chord Progressions

You can use Diminished Shapes like any other embellishment. This gives you a lot of flexibility where you can use it. It's common to use Diminished Shapes in the following ways.

Over ii V I's
Dmin7   G7(b9) | CMaj7 |

Over V's to I's
G7(b9) | CMaj7 |

Over I's
CMaj7 | CMaj7 |

So the bottom line is that it is common to use diminished everywhere, since you can resolve your ideas back to Chord Tones. You can also use it the same way you would use half steps and Circles to play notes that are not in your Key Center.

Diminished Can Be Very Simple

Diminished can be a lot simpler to play if you know what key your phrase is in. Just find out what major *key* you are in, and start on the 2nd degree of your scale.

2 3 4 5 b6 #6 7 #8 9

And then you can start Weaving and Noodling around with that scale.

2 3 2 3 4 5 4 5 b6 #6 b6 #6 7 #8 7 #8 9

Or go to the 5th scale tone, and up a half step (b6). It's the same scale. We are just starting in a different place.

5 b6 5 b6 5 4 3

5 b6 #6 7 #6 7 b6 5 4 3

Ascending:
2 3 2 3 4 5 4 5 b6 #6 b6 #6 7 #8 7 #8 9

Descending:
#8 7 #8 7 #6 b6 #6 b6 5 4 5 4 3 2 3 2

Add the half step below the first note, and you get the half - whole diminished.
b2 2 3 2 3 4 5 4 5 b6 #6 b6 #6 7 #8 7 #8 9

All super cool stuff!

Congratulations! That's It...

You made it through all the lessons in Bebop by the Numbers. Now what?

What's Next?

Now comes the fun part, it's time to develop your own ideas through the following exercises and putting this stuff to good use.

What follows next is a series of exercises, games and helpful examples, plus a growing catalog of "Riffs of the Day," our collection of ideas that you can use. Hopefully they will inspire you to develop your own.

Please note that the exercises that follow are not the definitive end-all, be-all. They are just a starting point that we hope will inspire you to develop your own ideas and extensions. These are a launching point, not a landing spot.

Be sure to check out BebopbytheNumbers.com for more examples, video tutorials, exercises and games.

Enjoy.

Danny

Exercises

The following exercises are designed to help you figure out how to build your own ideas, or "do it yourself" (DIY).

Exercise #1 - Stingers

Pick a Stinger, and play it over every chord in the blues, starting with beat one, and then changing which beat you play the Stinger on. You can then mix and match what beat you play the Stinger on. For example, beat one and beat four. Or how about beat two of the first measure, and beat one of the second measure?

Blues forms to start with:

Version One:
```
|   I    |   I    |   I    |   I    |
|   IV   |   IV   |   I    |   I    |
|   V    |   V    |   I    |   I    |
```

Version Two:
```
|   I    |   IV   |   I    |   I    |
|   IV   |   IV   |   I    |   I    |
|   ii   |   V    |   I    |   V    |
```

Version Three:
```
|   I    |   IV   |   I    |  v   I  |
|   IV   |  #iv°  |   I    |   VI    |
|   ii   |   V    | I  VI  | ii   V  |
```

Remember to keep the form, and change your Stingers to match your Chord Tones.

Exercise #2 - Pickups + Stingers

Try adding Pickups to Stingers and playing the blues. Here are some example ideas to try.

#2	3 1	`7	1 5	6	5 1
#2	3 5	#2	3 8	4	3 8
#4	5 1	7	8 5	4	3 1

A common question on playing these ideas over the blues is whether or not to play regular 7 in the scale, as opposed to the b7 in the scale, since it's a dominant chord. I would still play the regular 7th in these examples because it's a half step Pickup below the Chord Tone.

Next, try 2 Pickups.

2 #2	3 1	b6 `7	1 5	6 b6	5 1
2 #2	3 5	2 #2	3 8	5 4	3 8
4 #4	5 1	b6 7	8 5	5 4	3 1

Remember to keep the form, and change your Stingers to match your Chord Tones. These are not the complete list of combinations. Experiment and try to find them all.

Exercise #3 - Noodling

Try embellishing the Chord Tones of your song with half step approaches from below.

#23	`71	#45
#23 #23	`71 `71	#45 #45
#23 #23 #23	`71 `71 `71	#45 #45 #45
#23 #23 #23 #23	`71 `71 `71`71	#45 #45 #45 #45

Try variations and mix and match your Noodling. This is not the complete list of combinations.

#23 #45	`71 #23	#45 #23
#23#23#45	`71`71 #23	#45 #45 #23
#23#23#45#45	`71`71 #23#23	#45 #23 `71

The Goal "Focus on the Chord Tones and Noodle on them"

The goal is to be able to look at a chord progression, recognize the Chord Tones and patterns, and be able to noodle on those Chord Tones. Specifically, you can see Bb Major, know what your chord is, what the 3 is, and play something like #23, or #23 #23 `71

_____
_____
_____
_____
_____
_____
_____

Exercise #4 - Pickups + Noodling + Stingers

Try adding Pickups to Stingers to your Noodling ideas.

```
 #2 | 3#2 3#2 31           `#6`7 | 1`7 1`7 15
  2 | #23 #23 51           `6`#6 | `71 `71 35
2#2 | 3#2 3#2 35            4#4 | 5#4 5#4 53
`#6 | `71 `71 31             #4 | 5#4 5#4 51
```

Noodling and Shape Shifting Your "Noodling"

You can noodle your ideas over multiple measures in your song as chords change. Try creating long ideas.

```
(start on I chord )           #23 #23 #23 #23
(shift to next chord, IV)     #23 #23 #23 #23
(shift to next chord, I )     #23 #23 51
```

DIY - Do It Yourself

That is not the complete list of combinations. Experiment and try to find them all.

Remember the goal is to see the chord, know what the Chord Tones are, embellish and noodle with them, and end on a Stinger.

_____
_____
_____
_____
_____

Exercise #5 - Simple Scales

Try these ideas, playing the blues or another song. Keep the form and change your ideas to match your Chord Tones as they change with the progression of the song. Can you change your ideas to match major, minor, or diminished chords?

1 2 3 4 5   4 5 6 7 8

5 4 3 2 1   `6`7 1 2 3

Exercise #6 - Pickups + Simple Scales + Stingers

Try adding Pickups and Stingers.

`7 | 12 34 51   #23 | 45 67 8 3

#4 | 54 32 13   4#4 | 56 78 5 3

 3 | 45 67 85   4#4 | 54 32 1`5

`#5|`6`7 12 35   3 4 | 56 78 9 8

That is not the complete list of combinations. Experiment and try to find them all.

Exercise #7 - Pickups + Simple Scales + Noodling + Stingers

Put Pickups, Simple Scales, Noodling and Stingers together to create your own ideas.

2 | #23#23 #2345 6785

3 | 4567 8787 85

3 | 45#45 #4567 89 10 8

`#6|`71`71 2345 #45#45 31

4#4|5#45#4 5432 #23#23 51

#23|#23#4 5432 `71`71 31

Make your own ideas using these concepts.

Exercise #8 - Looping + Weaving + Stingers

Try these ideas, playing the blues or another song. Change your ideas to match the Major, Minor, or Diminished Chord Tones as they change with the progression of the song.

34 | 5434 5434 5678 53   1234 2345 3456 4567 85

1234 5345 6787 6543 31   1235 2346 3457 4568 5679 85

34 | 5678 7654 3212 31   3457 4568 3457 4568 5679 85

Make your own.

_____

_____

_____

_____

_____

_____

_____

_____

_____

_____

_____

_____

_____

_____

_____

Exercise #9 - Looping + Weaving + Noodling + Stingers

Try putting Looping, Weaving, Noodling and Stingers together.

34| 5#45#4 #23#23 4567 85

34| 5345 #45#45 6876 53

34| 5678 7878 #45 3454 3215

`71`71 2342 3453 4567 85

`71| #23#45 3456 5345 31

#45#45 3453 4567 85#45 31

Create your own ideas using Pickups, Looping, Weaving, Noodling and Stingers.

Exercise #10 - Circles

Here are some example ideas to try. Remember *half step below*, and *Scale Tone above*, Chord Tones.

#2 3 4 3

#4 5 6 5

#4 6 5

`7 2 1

#2 3 4 #2 3

`7 1 2 `7 1

4 #2 3

#2 4 #2 3

#4 6 #4 5

#2 4 3 #2 3

Create your own.

_____

_____

_____

_____

_____

_____

_____

_____

_____

_____

_____

_____

_____

Exercise #11 - Pickups + Circles + Stingers

Try adding Pickups and Stingers with your Circles.

2 | #23 43 53

4 | #45 65 #46 53

#46 | 5#4 5#4 51

`72 | `72 1#2 3#2 3#2 31

#23 | 4#4 5#4 56 53

`72 | 12 34 5#4 5#4 53

34 | #45 #23 #45 31

#24 | #23 #46 #46 53

23 | 4#4 6#4 6#4 51

34 | 56 #45 6#4 53

Do it yourself and make up your own ideas.

Exercise #12 - Circles + Everything Else So Far

2#2 | 3543 #2431 `7123 4#46#4 53

#24 | 31`71 2#24#2 3456 #4565 31

5678 | #456#4 5345 24#23 4567 85

Do it yourself. Make up your own using everything we've covered so far including Pick-ups, Stingers, Noodling, Looping, Weaving, Simple Scales and Circles.

Exercise #13 - Turns

Let's add Turns to our ideas using triplets and 16th notes.

(3 4 #4) 5 3   (4 #2 3) 5 1

(3 4 #4) 5 3 4#2 3 1   (3 1 5) 7 8 #4 5

 (1 3 5) 7 8   (#4 5 6) (#4 5 6) 5 3

`7 |(1 3 5) 7 8 #4 5   (#2 3 4)(#2 3 4) 3 1

                                 (#456#4)   5 3

(4 5 4 #2) 3 1   (3 5 7 9)   8 5

(2 4 3 5) 4 #2 3 1   (4542)(4542) 3 1

More Turns…

3 4 #4 5 3 4# 4 5 | (4 5 4 #2) 3 1

[rest] (4 5 4 #2) 3 1 [rest] | (4 5 4 #2) 3 1

[rest] (b7 8 b7 5) 6 5 [rest] | (b7 8 b7 5) 6 5

[rest] (3 4 3 1) 2 1 [rest] | (3 4 3 1) 2 1

Exercise #14 - Stretching Out

Try adding long notes to the middle of your ideas by stretching things out.

35_____ | 31

(,68) _____ 6#4 | (565) 31

#2 | 35 _____ | 3 1

(4 3 4) 35_____ #2 | 31

35_____ 6#4 | 53

6 8_____ 6 | 5 1

Write your own ideas with everything we've done so far. Stretching Out, Pick-ups, Stingers, Noodles, Weaving, Looping and Stingers.

_____
_____
_____
_____
_____
_____
_____
_____
_____
_____
_____
_____

Exercise #15 - Diminished

Try adding diminished shapes to your ideas (b6,#6,#8).

23 45 b6#6 7#8 9#8 7#6 b65 43 25

12 34 5b6 #6b6 54 31

12 34 5b6 #67 #87 #6b6 54 31

23 45 b6#6 7#8 9#8 7#6 b65 45 31

5b6 5b6 54 54 31

5b6 #67 #67 #6b6 #6b6 54 54 31

23 23 45 45 b6#6 b6#6 7#8 7#8 9#8 7#6 b65 45 31

#87 #87 #6b6 #6b6 54 54 32 32 35

5b6 #67 #6b6 53

(345) (b654) 31

(5b6#6) (7#6b6) 53

_____
_____
_____
_____

Exercise #16 - Embellishing Scale

Embellishments also work on scales, like these examples with half step embellishments on the 1 3 5 7 Chord Tones.

`7 1 2 #2 3 4 #4 5 6 #6 7 8 9

3 4 #4 5 6 #6 7 8 9

3 4 #4 5 3 4 #4 5 6 #6 7 8 9

2 #2 3 4 #4 5 6 #6 7 8 9

4 #4 5 6 #6 7 8 9

5 6 #6 7 5 6 #6 7 8 9

`7 1 2 #2 `7 1 2 #2 3 4 #4 5 6 #6 7 8 9

Exercising The Changes

To develop your ability to improvise, begin with changing how you approach improvising with each song and the chord changes.

Rule No. 1: We are figuring stuff out, so don't try to sound good… yet.

Rule No. 2: Only play the exercises below for ALL your solos, nothing else.

Step One: Figure out the form of the tune, the number of measures, phrases, etc.

Step Two: Figure out the Chord Tones and write them out (ie. 135 for each chord).

Step Three: Figure out the Key Centers and mark them. Underline your dominant chords.

Step Four: Play the following exercises in sequence, following the form of the tune. Play them in order and do the next step only when you can consistently play the step you are on. The examples are only references. Figure out your own ideas of each concept.

- Only play Stingers on Chord Tones (ie. 3 1) or (51) (15) (35)
- Next add Pickups (ie. #2 3 1) etc.
- Noodle with half step below Chord Tones (ie. #23 #23 #23) or (#45 #45 #45) etc.
- Half step arpeggios & variations (ie. `71 #23 #45 ) or (#45 #23 `71) (#45 #23 '71) etc.

Focus & Observe

The goal is to master the Chord Tones, and embellish the Chord Tones. That's it. Get really good at that. Do not play anything else on your solos until you master the Chord Tones. If you focus on it, it won't take long. Once you master the placement of these Chord Tones and embellishments you will gain the dexterity to create anything else. See where you are in two weeks of focused effort on this. You will be amazed.

Step Five: Continue with additional concepts.

- Simple Scales with Stingers (ie. 12 34 51) or (54 32 15)
- Weaving with Stingers (ie. 12 34 34 51) or (54 34 34 34 51)
- Looping with Stingers (ie. 12 34 53 45 31) or (12 34 51 24 31)
- Circles (ie. 5 #4 6 5) or (#4 6 #4 5) etc.

Step Six: Continue with more advanced ideas: Stretching it Out, Turns, Diminished Embellishments.

Examples

The following is an example of this exercise over blues.

Form: 12 Bar Blues, 3 four bar phrases
- 1 4 1 1, 4 4 1 1, 5 5 1 1

Key Centers for Concert, Bb and Eb Instruments

- Concert Bb, Eb & F (also the chord changes)
- Chords: Bb Major = Bb, D, F; Eb Major = Eb G Bb; F Major = F A C

- C Blues: C, F & G (also the chord changes)
- Chords: C Major = C E G; F Major = F A C; Gmajor = G B D

- G Blues: G, C & D (also chord changes)
- Chords: G Major = G B D; C Major = C E G; D Major = D F# A

Exercises to play over the form:

- Play on the beat each set of two 8th notes: (doo-dit)
  - 31, 51, 15, 13, 35, 38, 58
- On the off beat: (day-oo-dit)
  - #231, #235, #451, #453, 713, 715
- On the beat: (doo-day-oo-dit)
  - #2 3 #2 3, #4 5 #4 5, 7 1 7 1
- On the beat: (doo-day-oo-day-oo-dit)
  - #4 5 #4 5 #2 3, #2 3 #2 3 7 1

Experiment with more variations of your own:
- On the beat: #2 3 #4 5 #2 3 #4 5
- On the beat: 71 #23 #4 5
- On the beat: #45 #23 71

Next add Pickups to the above:
- Off the beat:
  - #2 3 #2 3 #2 3 1
  - #4 5 #4 5 #4 5 3
- Off the beat:
  - 7 1 #2 3 #4 5 3

Exercising Jazz Standards & Changes

Example work up of Jazz Standards. Circle the "key centers", underline the dominant chords, write the 3's and 5's of each chord. Try playing exercises one at a time over these chord changes, including Stingers, Pickups, Simple Scales, Looping, Weaving, Circles, Turns, and other ideas we have introduced.

Blue Bossa - Kenny Dorham

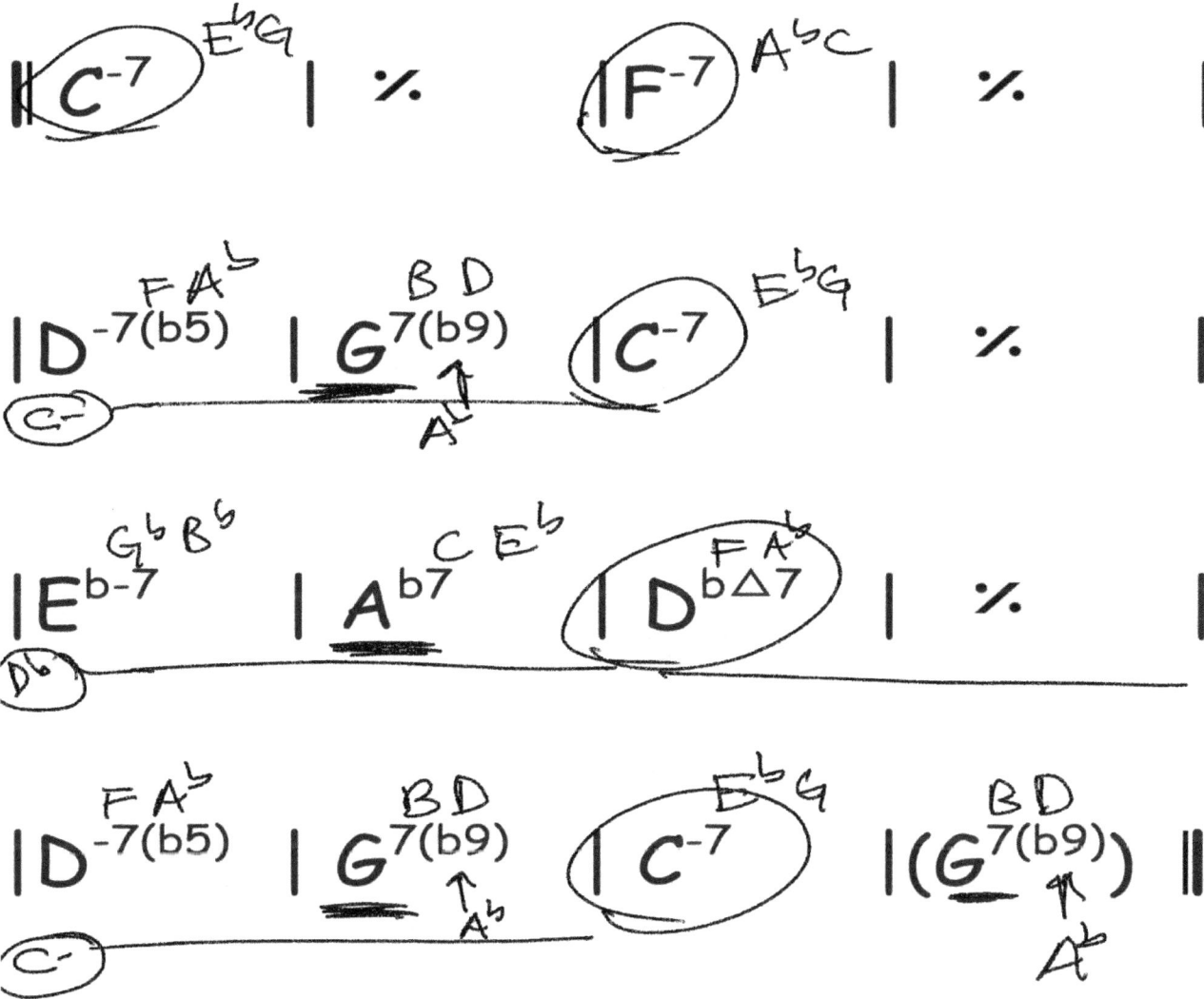

Blue Bossa has 2 main Key Centers, C minor and Db major. The first 8 bars are in C minor and then it shifts up to Db major for 4 measures, and back down to C minor for the last 4. For the F minor 7, you can either play C minor ideas, or play F minor. Both sound good.

Get more Standards Examples at BebopbytheNumbers.com.

Autumn Leaves by Joseph Kosma

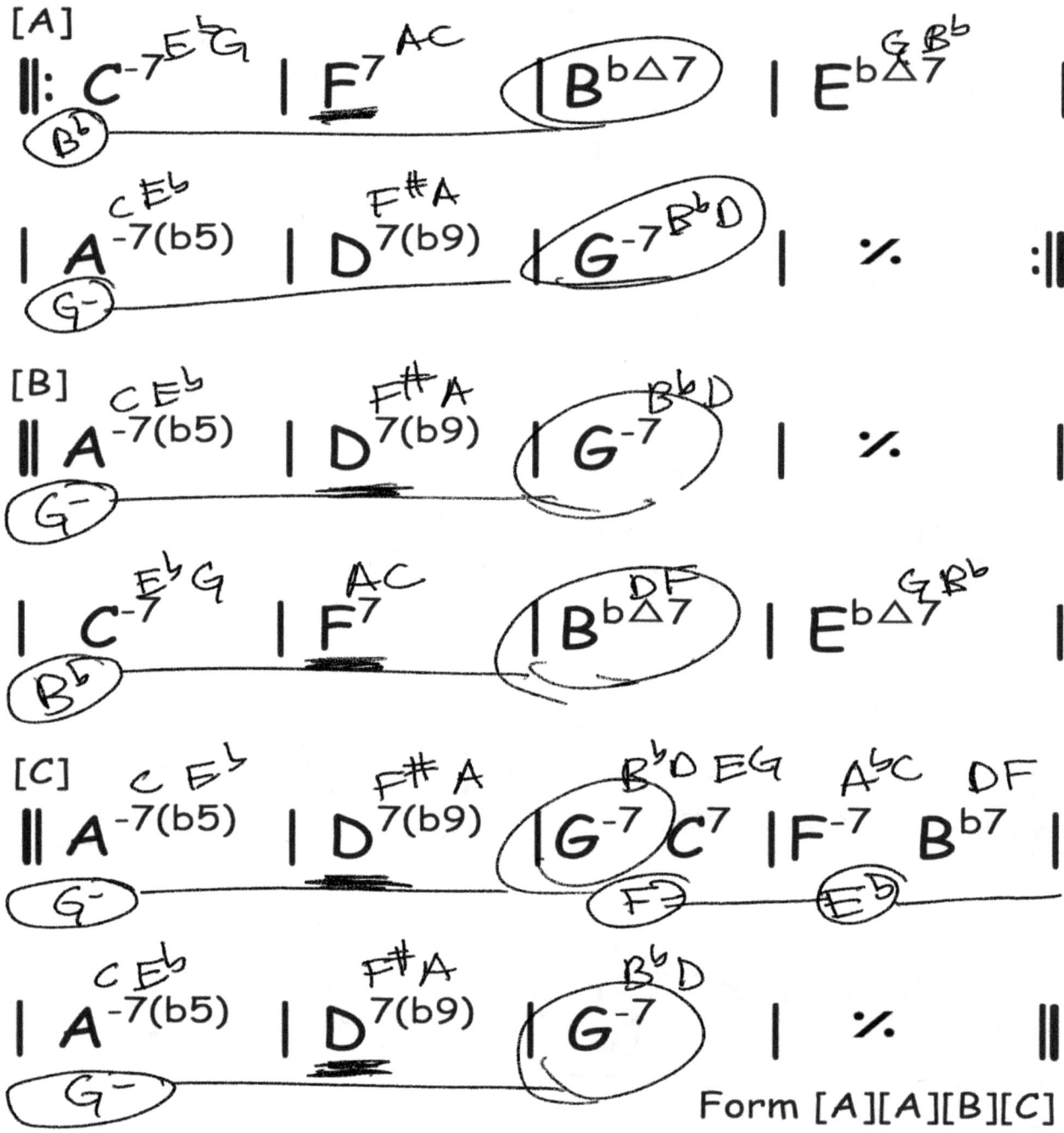

Autumn Leaves is largely in 2 Key Centers, Bb major and G minor featuring 251's in both. The Eb major is in the Bb Key Center, or you can play Eb ideas. The [A] is 251 in Bb, then 251 in G-. The [B] reverses that order, the [C] is 251 is Gminor with the turn around in the last 6 measures. Measure 3 & 4 of the [C] section is played many ways. This version has 2, 5 in F, and then 2 5 in in Eb and then G minor.

Get more Standards Examples at BebopbytheNumbers.com.

Take the A-Train - Billy Strayhorn

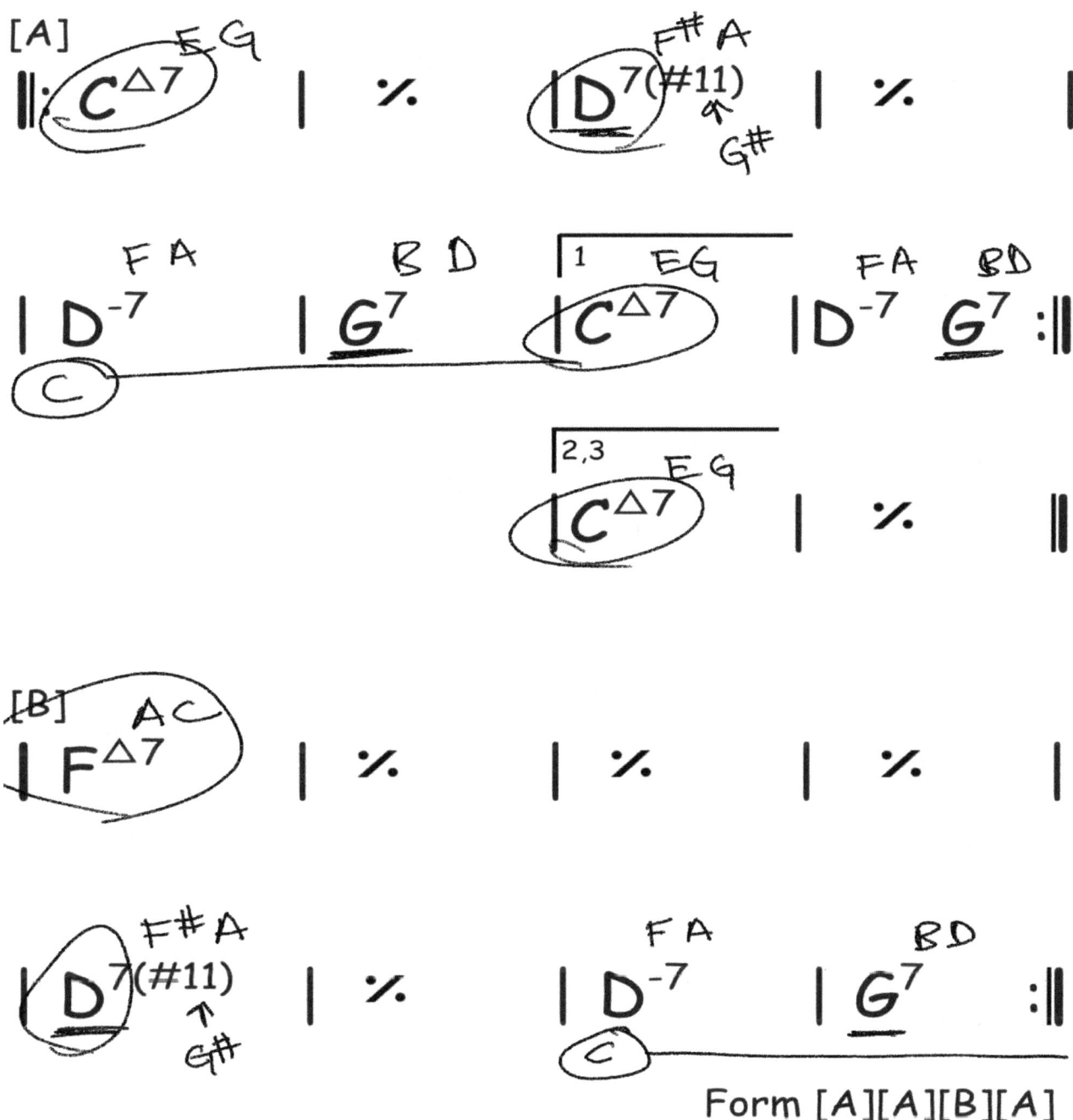

Take the A Train is largely in the C Key Center. The D7#11 is the 2 dominant (V of V).. play the F# and G#!! Then it's back to C. The bridge goes to the key of F, then back to our 2 dominant #11 (D)... and then 251 into C major.

Get more Standards Examples at BebopbytheNumbers.com.

Basic Blues

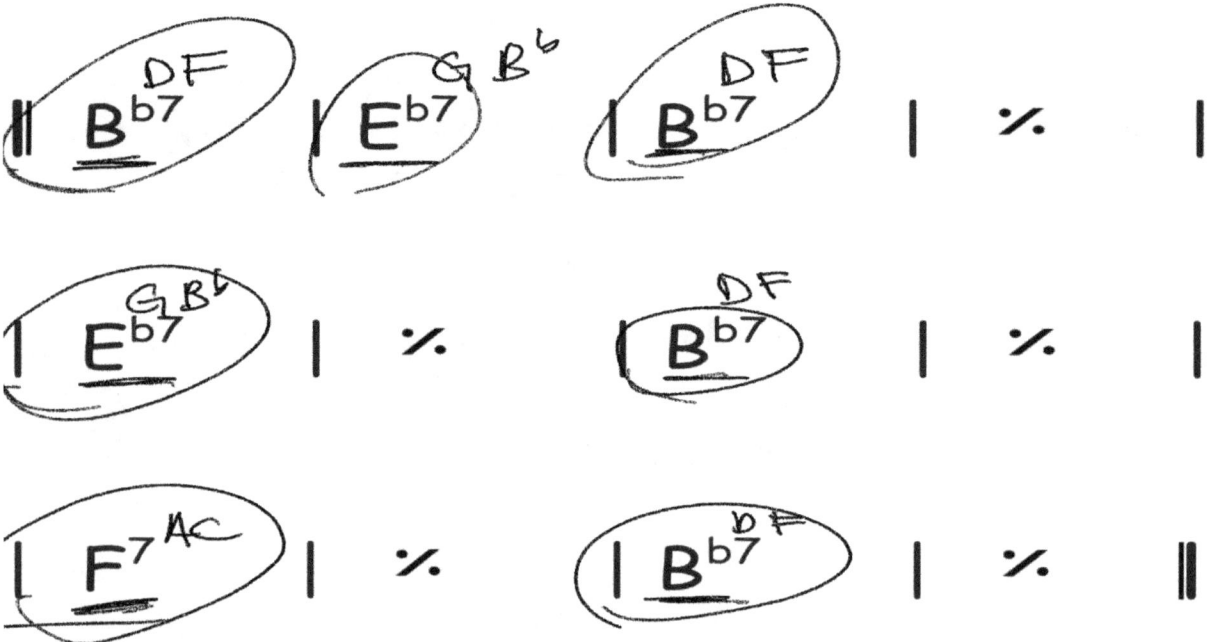

For Basic Blues play each change as a Key Center.

Blues - Common Changes

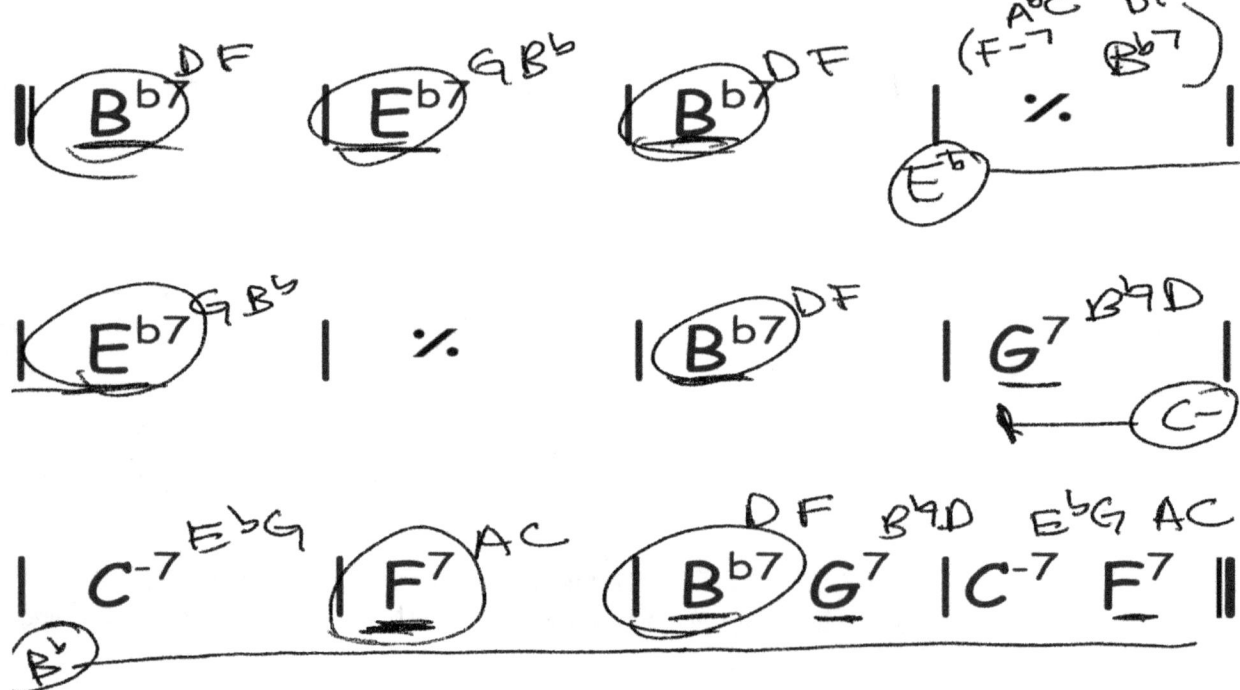

This is a more common blues progression including adding a 251 to the 4 chord (Eb). Play the 6 dominant in the key of C minor (or C major). And the last 4 you can either play in the Key Center of Bb, or play the F7 as a Key Center.

Rhythm Changes

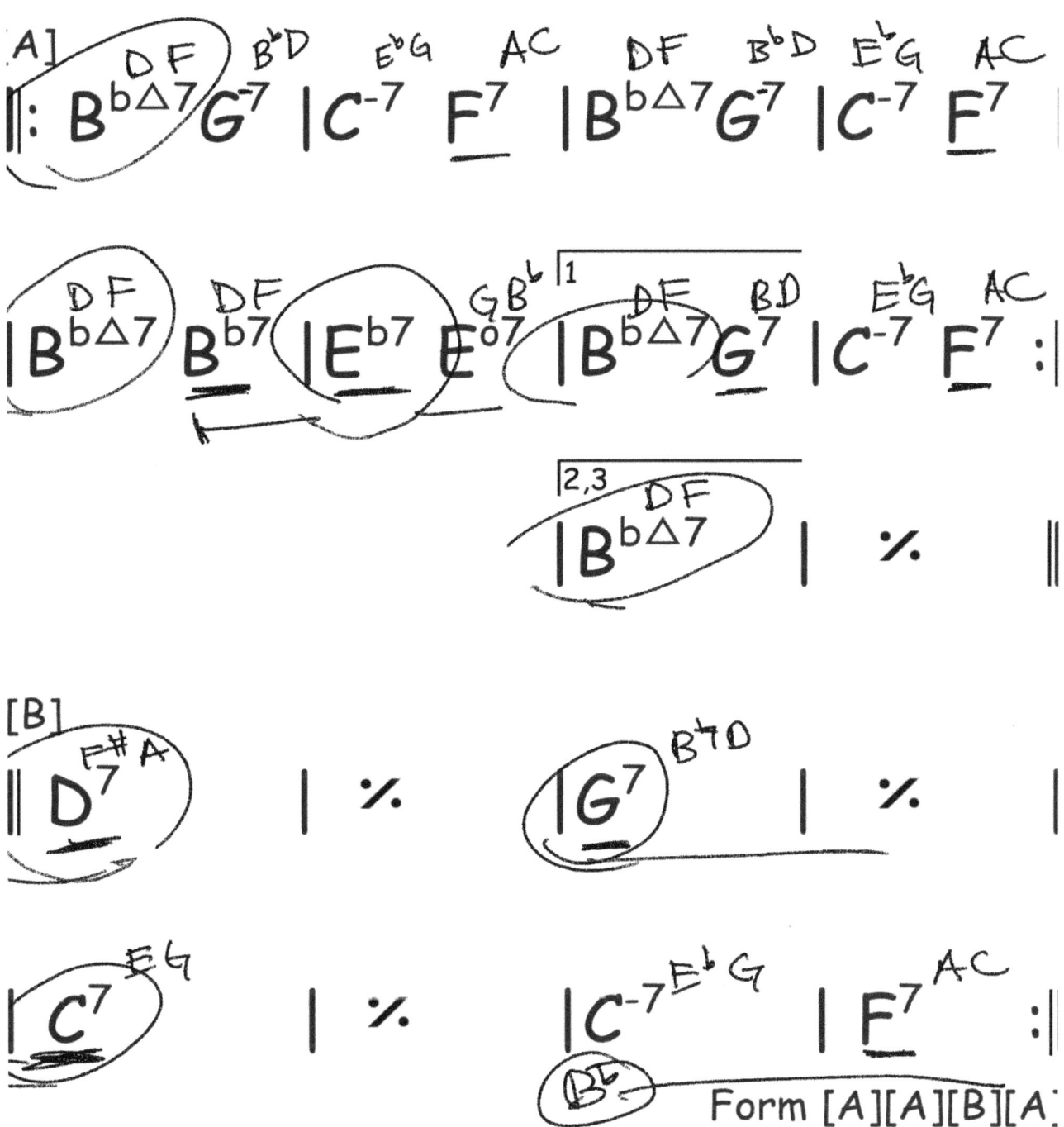

Rhythm Changes are another song with the AABA form. The [A] is largely in Bb in this example, briefly touching the 4 chord (Eb) before going back to Bb on the 1st and 2nd ending. The [B] section is dominant heavy with Key Centers for the 3 chord, 6 chord and 2 chord, before transitioning back to Bb with a 251. Also note that the [B] section, as 5 chords (dominants) lead to the next one in the sequence. D7 leads to G and then G7 leads to C. C7 is in the key of F, C7 is the V of V in Bb.

Get more Standards Examples at BebopbytheNumbers.com.

Game: The Noodling Game

The goal of this game is to develop a comfort level with the form of the song, the movement of the chord changes and simple rhythmic riffs that can be used in more advanced solos. This game works well in a big band setting as well as in small ensembles.

Rules

- Pick the form of the tune (i.e., 12 bar blues, rhythm changes, etc)
- Have the players identity Chord Tones for each chord
- Players will start by using patterns below and trade measures, starting with 1 measure, then 2, then 4.

Modes of play

- Musical chairs - go from player to player, trading a measure or a phrase and stop when someone makes a mistake. Restart from the player who made a mistake.

- Constant motion - do not stop when players make a mistake. Try to keep the momentum of the form going. Occasionally stop and ask the players where we are in the form.

Patterns

- Trade every measure, keeping the form, play over every chord change:
- Pattern One = #23 #23
- Teach them that they are embellishing the 3, by starting a half step below and riffing and resolving to the 3.
- You are starting on the embellishment, but the 3 is the goal
- Pattern Two = 3#2 3#2 3 1
- Teach them to use a Stinger at the end of the riff
- Starting on a Chord Tone and end with a Stinger
- Trade 2 bar phrases: keeping the form:
- Pattern Three = #23 #23 #23 #23 #23 #23
- Pattern Four = 3#2 3#2 3#2 3#2 3#2 31
- Free form: Still having the players follow the form, have them make up their own patterns
    - Ideas can be 2,4,6 or 8 notes, 8th notes.
    - Must use embellishments and 1,3 and/or 5
    - Each Player plays a measure, then rests a measure
    - Then the next player plays theirs.
    - Keep the form

Game: Connect the Dots

Pick a chord or song, and figure out these notes for your chords. Next connect any of these notes in a sequence. The only rule is to end on a chord tone. Use this to riff on blues and other chord changes. Experiment and make your ideas short and long, ie. 2 notes, then 4, 6, 8, etc. Try writing your patterns first and then play them.

Tip: Don't forget to try repeating notes and patterns.

Game: Connect the Dots (Minor)

Pick a chord or song, and figure out these notes for your chords. Next connect any of these notes in a sequence. The only rule is to end on a chord tone. Use this to riff on blues and other chord changes. Experiment and make your ideas short and long, ie. 2 notes, then 4, 6, 8, etc. Try writing your patterns first and then play them.

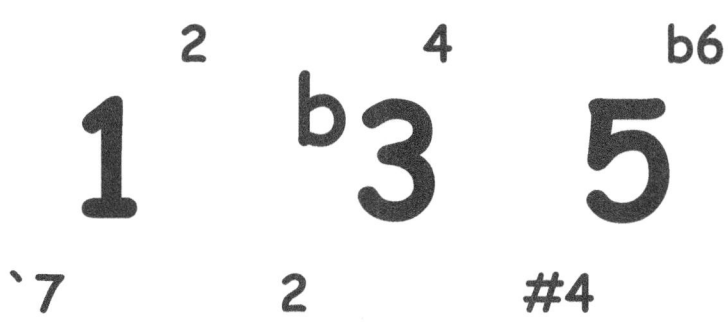

Tip: Don't forget to try repeating notes and patterns.

Game: Fill in the Blanks

Start with a rhythm, and a chord progression, then fill in the blanks with numbers. Remember to end on Chord Tones. If you repeat your phrases like this example, you may end up writing a really neat contrafact. Tip: If your rhythm ends of the 'and' of beat 4, choose chord tones from the next measure, i.e. beat 4 of measure 3 below.

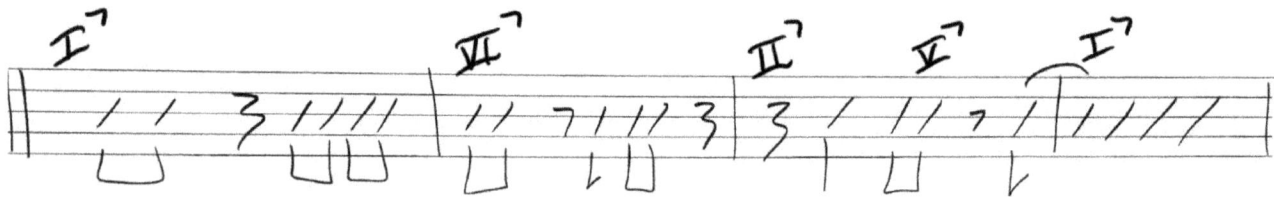

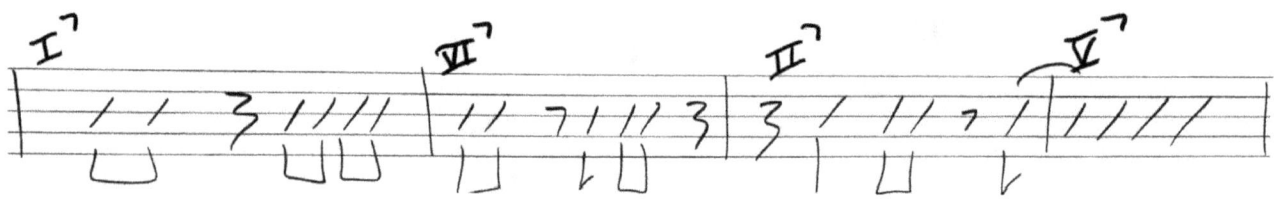

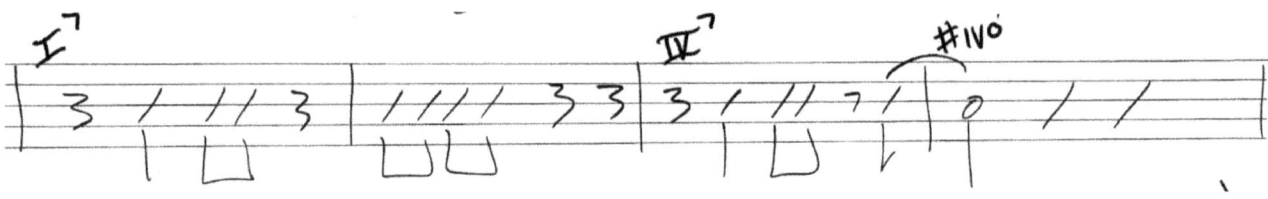

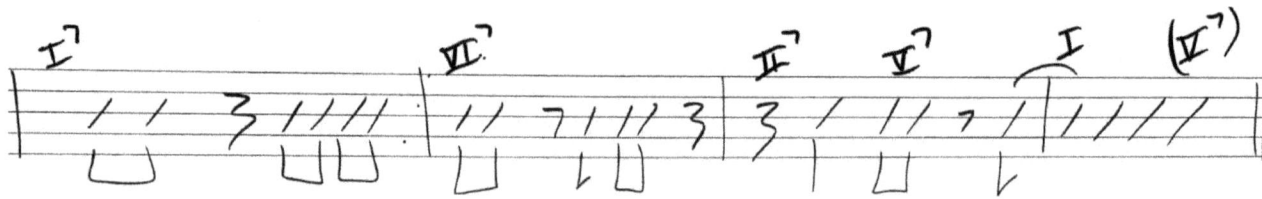

Get more examples at BebopbytheNumbers.com.

Game Dueling Circles

The goal of this game is to develop a comfort level with embellishing Chord Tones with Circles.

Rules

- Pick the form of the tune (i.e., 12 bar blues, rhythm changes, etc)
- Have the players identy Chord Tones for each chord in the form (135)
- Have the players figure out the Circle patterns for each Chord Tone
- Players will start by using patterns below and trading measures, starting with 2 measures, then 4, then 8.

Modes of play

- Musical chairs - go from player to player, trading a measure or a phrase and stop when someone does not end with a Stinger. Restart from the player who made a mistake.
- Constant motion - do not stop when players make a mistake. Try to keep the momentum of the form going. Occasionally stop and ask the players where we are in the form.
- Dueling Duets - have players split into twos and trade playing Circles for each other. Have one be the leader and the other the follower, copying the pattern of the Circle and which Chord Tones.
- Play the Cycle - write a series of patterns on the white board and play through the cycle every other measure, pattern 1, 2, 3 etc.

Circle Each Chord Tone

- 1 (and 8)
- 3
- 5
- 1 3 5
- 3 3 5
- 5 5 3
- 5 3 1
- 3 5 3

Example Patterns

- Under, Over   #2 4 3
- Over, Under   4 #2 3
- Under Thru Over   #2 3 4 3
- Over Thru Under   4 3 #2 3
- On Under Over (Mona Lisa)   3 #2 4 3
- On Over Thru Under   3 4 #2 3
- Doubling up Under   #2 4 #2 4 3
- Doubling up Over   4 #2 4 #2 3

Game: The Garbage Game

The goal of this game is to develop a comfort level with the form of the song, playing phrases that are not in the chord changes, and resolving them to chord changes. Whether by accident (aka mistakes) or on purpose, playing outside and resolving to Chord Tones is a very useful skill.

Rules

- Pick the form of the tune (ie 12 bar blues, rhythm changes, etc)
- Have the players identity Chord Tones for each chord (135)
- Players will start by using patterns below and trading measures, starting with 2 measures, then 4, then 8.

Modes of play

- Musical chairs - go from player to player, trading a measure or a phrase and stop when someone does not end with a Stinger. Restart from the player who made a mistake.
- Constant motion - do not stop when players make a mistake. Try to keep the momentum of the form going. Occasionally stop and ask the players where we are in the form.

Patterns

- Trade every 2 measures, keeping the form with the Stingers
    - Pattern One - just garbage
        - 2 eighth notes not using Chord Tones
        - If having problems playing wrong notes, play half step below or above Chord Tones
    - Pattern Two - 2 notes of garbage then closest Stinger
        - ie. #2#3 31
    - Pattern Three - repeat above patterns with 4 notes of garbage
    - Pattern Four - repeat with 8 notes of garbage
        - Note this becomes a two measure phrase
        - 8 notes outside + a Stinger (10 total notes)
        - Noodle on 8 notes outside (ie. #1#2#1#2 4 #4 4 # 4)
        - Then end on Stinger (ie. 53)
        - The Stinger is the goal, aka resolution
- Free form: Still having the players follow the form, have them make up their own patterns of garbage and length
    - Ideas can be 2,4,6 or 8 notes, 8th notes.
    - Must end on Stingers for 1,3 and/or 5
    - Decide how many measures for players to trade.
    - Keep the form
- Tip: if players are trading four measures, have them do 2 ideas. ie. Play an idea, rest, play another idea, rest, etc.

Tip: try having players use chromatic patterns for their garbage.

Game: DIY Game

The goal of this game is to develop a comfort level of having players make up their own ideas.

Rules
- Pick the form of the tune (i.e., 12 bar blues, rhythm changes, etc)
- Have the players identity Chord Tones for each chord (135)
- Pick a rule from the patterns below and have the players make up their ideas.
- Players will use the patterns they made up, trading measures, starting with 2 measures, then 4, then 8.

Modes of play
- Musical chairs - go from player to player, trading a measure or a phrase and stop when someone does not end with a Stinger. Restart from the player who made a mistake.
- Constant motion - do not stop when players make a mistake. Try to keep the momentum of the form going. Occasionally stop and ask the players where we are in the form.

Patterns
- Write 4 ideas, 4 eighth notes, must have #4, end on a Chord Tone
- Write 4 ideas, 5 eighth notes, must have #4, end on a Chord Tone
- Write 4 ideas, 7 eighth notes, must have #4 or #2, end on a Chord Tone
- Write 4 ideas, 8 eighth notes, must have #4 or #2, end on a Chord Tone

- Write 4 ideas, 7 eighth notes, must have #4 or #2, start with a Pickup, end on a Chord Tone
- Write 4 ideas, 8 eighth notes, must have #4 or #2, start with a Pickup, end on a Chord Tone

Tip: Create more rules using Circles, Turns, etc.

Bebop Prescription

Only play these ideas on every solo. Nothing else. Play one at a time. Do not play the next one until you master the previous. Play all of these on the downbeat. Play them all as eighth notes. There are no long notes in these patterns. Do this every day. Remember #2's are just 2's on minor chords, and #4's are just 4's on diminished.

- ☐ #23 #23
- ☐ #45 #45
- ☐ 12 34 51
- ☐ 12 34 53
- ☐ 35 42 31
- ☐ 53 42 31
- ☐ #45 #45 31

- ☐ #23 #23 51
- ☐ #46 5#2 31
- ☐ #46 5#2 43
- ☐ 35 4#2 31
- ☐ #23 #23 #45
- ☐ 12 34 53 #23

Extra Strength Prescription

Create your own patterns and play over your chord changes. Write them down. Start with 6 eighth notes, must include #4 or #2 and end on a Chord Tone.

- ☐ _____
- ☐ _____
- ☐ _____
- ☐ _____
- ☐ _____

- ☐ _____
- ☐ _____
- ☐ _____
- ☐ _____
- ☐ _____

Bebop by the Numbers Quick Reference

Stingers - Two eighth notes that can stand alone or be used to end your phrases. Basic Chord Tones always sound good. The 1 3 5 of your chord. 51, 15, 38, 35, 31

Pickups - As simple as one note added to the beginning of your idea, or longer by adding more notes to the front of your line. Half step below, or scale tone above always sounds good. #451, #235, 2#231

Noodling - Messing around with scale degrees by embellishing with half steps below the note over and over.
#23#23#23   #45#45#45

Simple Scales - Break scales into different sections, and then work on developing dexterity with different parts of the scale.
12345, 45678, 56789, 678910.

Weaving - Move back and forth through scales weaving on different parts of the scale.
3434 5454 3434 5454 31

Looping - Jumping around and repeating parts of the scale in order to extend ideas.
 1234 5345 3453 4531

Circles - "Circle" around and then land on a Chord Tone using a half step below, or a Scale Tone above. #243, 4#23, #2343, 43#23, #24#243, 4#24#23, 3#243, 34#23

Turns - add rhythmic embellishment and variety to your bebop lines to make your ideas more interesting. Start at the beginning of your lines with triplets and 16th notes. (3 4 #4) 5 3, (3 4 #4) 53 4#2 31,
(#4 5 6)(#4 5 6) 53

Stretching it Out - Try adding long notes in the middle of your ideas, and add Stingers at the end. 3 5_____ 6 #4 | 5 3,
or 6 8_____ 6 | 5 1

Blues Riffs - Riff on these ideas over Blues
#4555 #4555 4b3 4b3,
 b7 5 7 8, b3 1 b3 1,
b7 5 7 8, 42 #4 5,
 2 1 #2 3, (2 b3 2 1)
2 1, (6 b7 6 5) 6 5,
(b78 b75) 7 8 ,
(4#4 4b3) 4 b3

Diminished Shapes - Shortcut, play 4 notes of a minor scale, then up a half step and play 4 notes of that minor scale.

Half/Whole - Start on the five then go up a half step and play that diminished scale,
 5 b6 #6 7 #8 7 #6 b6 5.

Whole/Half - Start on the two, 2345 b6#6 7#8 7 #6 b6 5 4 5 3 1 (whole/half diminished).

Embellished Scale - play a scale but add half step embellishments on chord tones (1357),
`7 1 2 #2 3 4 #4 5 6 #6 7 8 9

Riff of the Day

Start your rehearsal with a Riff of the Day. You can try these patterns over the blues or other chord changes. Remember to keep the form, change the shape of the riff to match major, minor and diminished chords.

3 4 3 4 5 3 2 1 2 3

3 4 #4 6 5 3

3 4 #4 6 5 3 4 #2 3 4 3 1

#1 2 #2 3 4 #2 3 4   3 1

1 2 3 5 #4 5 3 1

5 4 3 `7 2 1

6 b6 5 `7 1 4 2 #2   3 1

#2 3 #2 3 2 1

#4   5 4 3 `7 2 1

4 5 6 8 7 6 5 3   4 2 3 `7 2 1

`7 2 4   5 `7 2 4 3 1 2 `7   1 `5

2 `7   1 2 3 4 5 6 #4 6 5 1

3 1

3 4 #4 6 5 #2 3 `7 2 1

#4   6 b6 5 3

2 4 3 5 3 1

3 4 5 b6 b7 b6 5 4   3 1

#4 5 3 4 2 3 1

#4   5 b6 #6 7 #8 7 #6 b6   5 3

1 4 3 #2 3 1

1 `7 1 2 3 1 #4 6 5 3

1 2 3 4 #4 6 5 3 4 #2 3 `7 2 1

3 4 #4 6 5 3 4 #2 3 1

7 6 4 #4 5 1

1 3 2 1 4 #2 3 5

5 4 2 #2 3 1

#4 6 5 4 3 #1 2 4 3 1

#4 6 5 2 4 #2 3 `7 2 1

3 4 #4 5 4 3 #2 3 2 1

`7 1 2 5 3 1

5 4 `6 1 3 2

6 8 b7 #4 6 5

1 2 4 #2 3 5 6 #4 5 3 4 `7 2 1

2 `7 1 4 #2 3 6 #4 5 3

6 5 4 #2 3 1

`7 1 #2 3 #4 6 5 3 2 1

2 `7 1 4 #2 3 6 #4 5 3

5 #4 4 #4 5 4 #2 4 3 1

2 4 #4 6 5 3 4 5 3 1

#8 7 #8 7 #6 #5 #6 #5 5 4 5 4 3 2 3 2

2 4 6 #4 5 3 4 #2 3 `7 2 1

5 #4 4 2 #2 3 `7 2 1 `5

5 3 4 5 3 7 6 5 3 2 1 3 5 2

6 #4 5 1

`7 1 2 #2 3 4 #4 5 6 5

2 `7 1 3 2 b3 b6 4 b5 7 b6 6 9 7 8 5

7 6 7 6 b6 b5 b6 b5 4 b3 4 b3 2 1 2 1

5 b6 b7 b8 b9 b8 b7 b6 5

2 3 4 5 #5 #6 7 #5 5 3

Get more Riff's of the Day at BebopbytheNumbers.com.

Common Chord Progressions

If you take the time to notice, you will see and hear recurring patterns in music of the same progressions of chords. There are many "common" patterns to look for in Chord Progressions:

	Progression	Plain English
1	I IV I	1 4 1
2	I V I	1 5 1
3	I IV V I	1 4 5 1
4	I vi IV V	1 6 4 5
5	I vi ii V	1 6 2 5
6	I IV ii V	1 4 2 5
7	I II7 ii V I	1 2 7 2 5 1
8	I IV iii vi ii V I	1 4 3 6 2 5 1
9	I VII7 bVII7 VI7 ii V I	1 7 b7 6 2 5 1
10	I iii IV #ivo V vi ii V I	1 3 4 #4 5 6 2 5 1
11	I v I7 IV	1 5 minor, 1 4
12	I II7 ii V I	1 2 dominant, 2 5 1
13	I viio iii vi	1 7ø, 3 6
14	I #ivo IV iii vi ii V7 I	1 #4o, 4 3 6 2 5 1
15	ii V I	2 5 1
16	II7 ii V I	2 dominant, 2 5 1
17	II7 V7 I7 VI7	2 5 1 6 (all dominant)
18	ii(b5) V i	-2(b5) 5 -1 (minor 251)
19	iiø V7 i	2ø 5 -1 (minor 251)
20	ii V I vi	2 5 1 6
21	V IV I	5 4 1
22	III7 VI7 II7 V7	3 6 2 5
23	IV iv bVII7 I	4 4 minor, b7, 1
24	#ivo IV iii biii ii V7 I	#4o, 4, 3, b3, 2 5 1

dom = dominant, o = diminished, Ø = half diminished

About the Author - Danny Kolke

Jazz Musician, Pianist, Composer, Arranger, Educator, Jazz Club maker, Music Teacher, Husband and Father of Three, and former tech entrepreneur…

As a Jazz pianist, Danny Kolke is known for his aggressive technique, passionate voicings and hard swinging blues and gospel feel. As Jim Wilke (KNKX / Jazz After Hours Public Radio International) has said, "if you like trio's like those of Oscar Peterson and Gene Harris, you are going to like this trio." Danny plays piano regularly at Boxleys in North Bend and he has four CD's on the Pony Boy Records label. His most recent CD, "When You're Smiling" is a hard-swinging traditional piano trio album with some new twists, a must have. Danny's previous album "Danny Kolke Trio +One Featuring Pete Christlieb", add's Pete's amazing legendary Tenor sound to the dynamic group. Danny's other Trio recordings are "Sunday Nights, Live at Boxley's" and "A New Meaning".

As an educator, Danny has been teaching Jazz improvisation to students for fourteen years in a variety of group formats as well as private lessons. Known for making improvisation fun and approachable, Danny works with students of all ages from the very young to the young at heart.

Jazz Club & Restaurant
In 2009, Danny founded Boxley's jazz club in North Bend Washington" which became known around the world ranked as one of the best Jazz clubs in the world according to Downbeat Magazine 7 years in a row. Boxleys was an amazing and almost magical place from the day it opened until 2016 when they decided to close its doors and focus on the nonprofit organization. In 2018 Boxleys reopened in its current location as a performance venue.

Nonprofit Organization
In 2010, Danny founded the Boxley Music Fund (now JazzClubsNW), a nonprofit 501c3 based organization committed to helping support live music performance and Jazz education. JazzClubsNW is a membership based organization that pays musicians to host clinics and workshops, public performances as well as organize Jazz & Blues festivals across the Northwest including sponsoring Jazz nonprofits in Bellingham and Tacoma Washington as well as launching Jazz Festivals in Tacoma, Olympia, North Bend and Edmonds.

Now Former Tech Entrepreneur
As a Technology Entrepreneur, Danny founded his software company in 1999 and led the organization for 16 years from a start-up to being publicly traded. Danny is named on five patents and achieved recognition as one of the most influential people on the internet for writing CRM for Google. In 2016, Danny went to work for Microsoft, and in 2018, Amazon Web Services (AWS). June 2021, Danny logged out of his corporate laptop to focus on music first, and making time for other projects.

On A Personal Note

So I made another big jump on June 15th, 2021, I logged out of my work laptop for the last time. I decided that life is too short to not do what I love, so it is time for me to leave corporate America, and I am going to be a musician, first. I am going to teach more piano, pick up more gigs, practice and write music. Record more. Start a recording studio for my favorite jazz artists. Run a jazz festival and a blues festival. Run the non-profit I started 13 years ago. And maybe when I get bored, or need to fill some gaps, pick up some part-time work by helping people I care about with their businesses.

Although the world of tech has been good to me, it's music that I love. I believe God put this gift in my heart, and I am going to give it the proper attention it deserves. Let me know if you want a piano player for a gig, a crazy jazz piano teacher, or if you want help starting a Jazz club or festival, or if you want me to tell you what you are doing wrong with your company.

I hope you are doing what you love to do, today!

-danny

dannykolke.com

More Bebop

For more information on Bebop by the Numbers and ideas for what you can do with these concepts, check out our website at BopbytheNumbers.com.

For Danny's Riffs of the Day, follow him on instagram instagram.com/dannykolke.

Bebop by the Numbers
Copyright 2023 Kolke Media LLC
All Rights Reserved

No part of this book may be reproduced without written consent from Danny Kolke and/or Kolke Media LLC.

Kolke Media LLC
PO Box 493
North Bend, WA 98045
BopbytheNumbers.com
DannyKolke.com

Cover Artwork Gifted by Nicole Tastad.
An Original Painting by Nick Maes (1945- 2004)

A Very Special Thank You to

Ray & Des Kolke
Greg Williamson
Matso Limtiaco
Michael Glynn
Jon Hamar
Chris Symer
Pete Christlieb
Jay Thomas
Steve Treseler
Jared Hall
Matt Wenman
Bill Leather
Haley Isaacs
Hannah Mowry
Kelly Eisenhour
Tom Daniels & Karen Rabideau
Bill Stewart
Bob Bauman & Audrey Paisley
Gary Schwartz
Patrick Davis
Nicole Tastad
David Cook
Bob Thordarson

My Jazz Band Students
My Private Lesson Students
Members of JazzClubsNW
Gene Harris, Dizzy Gillespie & Oscar Peterson
Ray Price & Chris Clark
The Byford, Bruce & Kolke Families
My Parents Daniel & Selma
Leslie, James, Daniel III and Robyn

www.ingramcontent.com/pod-product-compliance
Lightning Source LLC
Chambersburg PA
CBHW081257170426
43198CB00017B/2826